# Eat In Color!

*Colorful & Delicious Recipes from my Heart*

By
Chef Renée Williams

# Dedications & Acknowledgements

This book is dedicated to you, my readers, my friends, my family, my loved ones. I care about you. You might not know me, but I know you and can say from my heart that I love you. I love you enough that I thought it my duty and responsibility to share with you something I know will change your life for the better. What I know are the keys to a happier, healthier and more colorful life! "Eat in Color!" is one of, hopefully, many more cookbooks created to get you started in adding more colorful creations on your plate.

I would also like to recognize my wonderful husband without whom this book would not have been possible. Thank you for pushing, encouraging and loving me and all my colorful ways! You truly make my sun brighter, my moon closer, my heart beat faster and my laughter more joyful. I love you around the universe and back (twice, no three times)! Lol

To my children, Christina, Christopher and Haven, you are my rhythm. Without you all I could not dance. Thank you for being you and keeping me dancing.

To my mother, my Poppy, my dad, sisters and brothers. With you guys, love really is as it should be, unconditional and infinite. I am grateful for you all. Thank you. A special thanks to my sister Jackie. Whew! I have had a lot of crazy business ideas and you (and Kenneth) have supported me with them all! Thanks for always encouraging me and pushing me on. Annette thanks for the TT (testimony times)!

Thanks to WinTV and all the staff and volunteers for helping me produce a great television show! I love and thank each of you: Vivi, Mike, Justin, Dee, Howard, Patti, Jenny and every intern who worked on the show past, present and future. Thanks to the Simply Chef Renée (SCR) Team, Angela Spence, Joyce Hudson and Greg Burack! You all rock and I am so grateful for you.

Thanks for all you do all the time!

# Introduction

Talk about wearing your heart on your sleeve, here's mine on a plate! First, please allow me to thank you for picking up this copy of "Eat in Color!" I truly appreciate you, your support and your interest in my endeavor.

I wrote "Eat in Color!" with you in mind and it comes directly from my heart. I am so excited to share my passion for food and my desire to bring back the true joy of cooking at home and sharing a meal with the people you love and care about. There are so many things I want to say, but I'll do my best to keep it short and to the point.

I conduct a lot of research, not just for recipes and culinary trends, but on foods that have a positive effect on our health and our very lives. I will start with this, I know that eating and cooking with fresh ingredients, hearty amounts of plant-based foods, seasoned well and cooked with a light hand will not only delight your eyes but will electrify your taste buds and improve your overall health. This I know for sure.

It is well documented that eating a more colorful plant-based diet is better for you. I believe that eating the right foods, those your body requires to function properly, not only can prevent diseases but it can also generate good health and an overall positive feeling of well-being for you both physically and mentally. Who doesn't want that! Furthermore, I found that research involving the study of diet, nutrition and diseases, such as cancer, high blood pressure and diabetes just to name a few, that one conclusion which seems to be consistent across the board is that a more colorful, plant-based diet along with exercise and drinking plenty of water can do significantly more for you and your body than any medication, diet or surgery. I love this! While in this cookbook you will find meat dishes (sorry Mr. Chicken, Mr. Cow and Mr. Pig) they are surrounded by colorful sides that should cover more than two-thirds of your plate! They are recipes I developed from my travels, research, experiences and some I just happened to fall upon while tinkering in my kitchen.

Use them! Change them! Take them to potlucks! Just incorporate more color into your diet and enjoy the life you were meant to live. Good nutrition is a powerful gift which you can give yourself. I encourage you to use this book to help you prepare delicious, nutritious and colorful meals I'm sure will change your life forever!

# The Power of Eating in Color

As a registered dietitian for over 13 years, I can say with confidence that eating in color is not just visually appealing, but it's also very beneficial for the body, mind and spirit. The colors of food indicate the pigmentation of the molecules that make up the food itself. Colors like red found in apples, watermelon and tomatoes come from a pigment called Lycopene. Lycopene has been associated with anti-cancer fighting properties called antioxidants. Anthocyanins is another red colored pigment antioxidant associated with protecting cells and helping to protect the heart from damage. Studies have revealed that this antioxidant is very effective against fighting colon cancer. In my professional opinion, the more colored foods you can add to your daily diet, the more potential benefits you are giving your body.

I've worked with clients and patients ranging from children to adults who are living well into their 90's and even 100's. One of my main recommendations is eat a variety of foods, particularly fruits and vegetables because they provide: color, fiber, water, vitamins, minerals and properties that help protect our many vital organs and cells. A good rule of thumb is aim to eat lots of fruits and vegetables and to eat in season. Try apple or berry picking in the fall and summer to get a better appreciation of the environment of the fruit and how they grow. The more we are in touch with the source of our food, the more we can develop a deeper appreciation for how natural foods benefit our bodies.

This book, "Eat in Color!" by Johnson and Wales graduate, Chef Renée, is a wonderful example of a cookbook that emphasizes the importance of eating in color because of the health benefits color provides. Some of the recipes are amazingly simple, yet they are incredibly delicious while others will test your kitchen skills. Chef Renée guides you step-by-step in incorporating more taste into healthier dishes for daily meals.

I love Chef Renée because she is an advocate for healthy but deliciously tasting foods. She has put her heart and passion into this book from a place of love and personal experience with the loss of a loved-one due to breast cancer. She wants to convey to you, her beloved readers, the best way to prepare and eat delicious tasting foods in color!!!!

*Mara*

With gratitude and to the best health,


Mara Davis, MS, RD, CD-N, LDN
Registered Dietitian

# Appetizers

Feta, Cranberry & Fresh Basil Crostini 3

Pesto, Basil & Cheese Crostini 5

Salmon & Avocado Poppers 8

Spiced Corn & Vegetable Stuffed Tomatoes 9

Crab Cakes 11

Tacos 13

Rack of Lamb 16

# Feta, Cranberry & Fresh Basil Crostini

Ingredients
1 pound feta cheese, crumbled
1 to 1½ cup dried cranberries, chopped
1 bunch of fresh basil, chiffonade
Hot red pepper and garlic infused olive oil, to taste
Kosher salt
Fresh ground black pepper
Roasted grape tomatoes (see below)
Crostini

Method of Preparation
1. In a large bowl, add feta, cranberries, basil and olive oil. Fold together using a rubber spatula being careful not to smash the feta.
2. Season with salt and fresh ground pepper.
3. To serve: Spread cheese mixture atop crostini. Add roasted tomato and garnish with a small basil leaf.

Optional: Dried cherries can be substituted for the cranberries for another great taste.

Roasting the Tomatoes
Preheat oven to 400°F.
Cut the tomatoes in half. Place the tomatoes with the cut side up on a parchment lined baking sheet.
Whisk together olive oil, white balsamic vinegar, kosher salt and fresh ground pepper.
Drizzle oil mixture over tomatoes and roast until tomatoes are softened and flavorful.

Making the Crostini
Preheat oven to 400°F.
Slice 1 baguette into ¼ inch pieces. Lay slices flat onto a parchment lined baking sheet and drizzle with oil. Toast in the oven for 12 to 15 minutes or until golden brown.

# Pesto, Basil & Cheese Crostini

*This is really one of the "house favorites," meaning I always have these ingredients in the house and can make them as a snack while waiting for dinner or whip them up quickly if unexpected company drops by. I hope it becomes one of your house favorites!*

Ingredients
1 baguette sliced about ¼ inch thick
1/4 cup butter, melted
Garlic infused olive oil
1 clove garlic, roasted and smashed
¼ cup pesto
Gruyere cheese, shredded
Parmesan cheese, shredded
Fresh ground black pepper
Red bell pepper, diced

Method of Preparation
1. Preheat oven to 400ºF.
2. In a bowl add butter and 2 tablespoons of olive oil.
3. Brush the bread slices with olive oil mixture. Bake in the oven until golden brown and crispy.
4. Add smashed garlic to pesto and mix together.
5. Spread the mixture onto the bread. Top with cheeses and black pepper.
6. Bake until cheese is melted and bubbling. Remove and sprinkle with red pepper.

# Salmon & Avocado Poppers

Ingredients
2 avocados
Juice of 3 limes
6 ounces of smoked salmon
4 boiled eggs, crumbled
8 pieces of bacon, cooked and crumbled
One bunch of fresh dill, stems removed
Kosher salt, to taste
Fresh ground black pepper, to taste
Creamy Chipotle Sauce (see index)

Method of Preparation
1. Juice the limes and set aside.
2. Cut avocado in half and remove the seed. Once the seed is removed, cut each half into 2 wedges. Cut each wedge in half horizontally making two "squares" or "poppers." Line up each popper onto a baking sheet or work top area.
3. Brush each avocado piece thoroughly with lime juice using a pastry brush. Sprinkle with a little salt if desired.
4. Squirt a dab of the Creamy Chipotle Sauce in the center of each avocado piece, then lay a strip of smoked salmon on top. The sauce will act as a glue.
5. Drizzle infused olive oil on salmon. Sprinkle with fresh ground black pepper.
6. Top with egg, bacon and fresh dill.
7. Place on a serving platter.

Note: Leaving the skin on the avocados for this dish makes it easier for guest to pick it up without making a mess; however, these may be presented individually (or as a pair) with avocado skins removed.

# Spiced Corn & Vegetable Stuffed Tomatoes

Ingredients

15 small tomatoes halved horizontally
2-3 ears of corn
1 English cucumber, diced
1 medium red onion, diced
2 celery stalks, diced
2 mangoes, peeled, seeded and diced
¼ cup feta cheese, crumbled
Chipotle Sour Cream
Fresh basil
Fresh c ilantro
Kosher salt
Fresh ground black pepper

Pinch of red pepper flakes
Extra virgin olive oil

Champagne & Mango Vinaigrette (See index)

Method of Preparation

1. Preheat broiler on medium-high heat. Place the rack between 4 and 6 inches from the top.
2. While waiting for the broiler to heat, carefully slice a thin layer from the bottoms of the tomatoes so they sit flat on a foil-lined baking sheet. Set each half upright and scoop out the seeds leaving flesh in the bottoms and inside.
3. Brush with a little olive oil and sprinkle with salt and pepper.
4. Place under the broiler and char just a bit. This will take about 2 to 2½ minutes so watch carefully and remove while the tomatoes are still firm. Set aside and allow to cool.
5. Shuck the corn and remove the silks if you have not already. Remove the kernels and place in a large bowl. Add the onion, red pepper flakes and a drizzle of oil. Toss and place on a baking sheet lined with foil and place under the broiler to char shaking the pan as needed. Again, this is a quick cook so keep an eye on the corn. Cook for 3 minutes. When charred, remove and allow to cool.
6. In a large bowl, add cucumber, celery, basil, cilantro and mangoes. Squeeze a little of the vinaigrette into the bowl and mix adding salt and pepper to taste.
7. Fold in cooled corn and onion mixture.
8. Add a dollop of sour cream inside the tomato and then stuff each tomato with the vegetable mixture. Add chipotle sauce to the sour cream to create Chipotle Sour Cream.
9. Squirt a little of the vinaigrette atop, garnish with cilantro sprinkles and serve.

# Crab Cakes

Ingredients

1 pound lump crab meat
2 large eggs
2½ tablespoons mayonnaise
1½ teaspoons Dijon mustard
1 teaspoon Worcestershire sauce
¾ teaspoon Old Bay seasoning
Pinch of red pepper flakes
½ teaspoon capers, chopped
1 teaspoon dill, chopped

¼ cup celery, finely diced
¼ cup shallots, sautéed
1½ tablespoon parsley, chopped
½ cup panko
Canola oil
3 tablespoons clarified butter
Lemon wedges

Method of Preparation

1. Open the crab meat and check for shells or hard pieces by gently rubbing fingers together. Try to preserve large chunks for the cakes. Once done, set the prepared crab meat aside.
2. Line a baking sheet with parchment paper. I like to brush it with a light coat of butter.
3. In a large bowl, whisk the eggs. Add the mayonnaise, mustard, Worcestershire, Old Bay, red pepper flakes, capers, dill, celery, shallots and parsley. Mix together.
4. Gently fold in the crab meat and panko until combined. Shape into small cakes and place on the baking sheet. Cover with plastic wrap and place in the refrigerator for at least 1 hour or more.
5. Preheat a large nonstick pan to medium heat and drizzle with canola oil and butter. When the butter is bubbly, gently place crab cakes into the pan. Cook until golden brown for 3 to 5 minutes. Turn and cook on the other side until brown.
6. Continue cooking until they are golden brown. Serve with Tartar Sauce or Spicy Remoulade Sauce, hot sauce or a lemon wedge.

Easy Tartar Sauce:
In a large bowl combine 1 cup of mayonnaise, 1½ tablespoon of sweet relish, ½ tablespoon of chipotle sauce (optional), ¾ teaspoon of Dijon mustard and fresh squeezed lemon juice. Add in the lemon juice a little at a time tasting after each addition.

# Tacos

Ingredient
Cod Marinade
3 tablespoons siracha
3 tablespoons canola oil
3 tablespoons fresh cilantro
1½ tablespoon soy sauce
1 garlic clove, minced
¼ teaspoon Old Bay seasoning
¼ teaspoon paprika
Juice of ½ lime
Pinch of sugar
1 pound cod

Chicken Marinade
2 tablespoons dijon mustard
2 garlic cloves, chopped
2 orange slices
2 lemon slices
1½ tablespoons olive oil
1 tablespoon sesame oil
1 tablespoon Worcestershire sauce
1 tablespoon sugar
2 sprigs of thyme
1 sprig of rosemary
½ teaspoon salt

¼ teaspoon fresh ground pepper
1 pound chicken breast, bite-sized pieces

Pork Belly
Cut pork belly in chunk or bite size pieces

1-package small corn tortillas

Toppings
2 cups kale & cabbage slaw
1 small red cabbage, chopped
1 bunch of romaine lettuce, torn
3 tomatoes, seeded and diced
1 to 2 jalapenos, sliced (seeded if desired)
1 carrot, julienned
2 radishes, julienned
Pineapple or mango, diced
Fresh cilantro
Lime wedges

Creamy Chipotle Sauce (See index)

Champagne and Mango Vinaigrette (See index)

Method of Preparation
1. Make marinade for cod. In a large plastic bag add the first nine ingredients (siracha through the sugar). Seal the bag and shake vigorously. Add the cod and turn the bag gently a few times. Marinate for 15 minutes.
2. In a separate bag, add olive oil, bourbon seasoning, paprika, salt and pepper. Seal and mix. Add the chicken and squeeze to coat. Set aside to marinate.
3. Make the marinade for the chicken. Add all the ingredients for the chicken marinade in a plastic bag (except chicken), seal and squeeze all ingredients together and smash around to thoroughly mix. Add chicken pieces and coat. Set aside to marinate.
4. Heat a cast iron skillet. Add the pork belly and cook until crispy. Remove to a paper-towel lined plate. Keep warm.

5.  Pour off all but 1 tablespoon of the rendering. Remove the chicken from the marinade.
    Discard the marinade and cook the chicken until golden brown. Set aside and keep warm.
6.  In a clean pan, heat oil. Remove fish from marinade and pat lightly to remove excess liquids. Cook fish
    for 3 to 4 minutes on each side until done. (Times may vary depending on the thickness of your fish.). Set aside.
7.  Heat tortillas on both sides. Remove to a dish and cover with a damp, clean dish towel.
8.  For service: In one taco spread your sauce, add your protein (fish, chicken or pork) and add
    any of the fresh toppings. End with a dollop of the chipotle sauce. The combinations are endless!
    Garnish with fresh cilantro and lime.

# Rack of Lamb

Ingredients
8 lamb loin chops
3 garlic cloves,
2 tablespoons extra-virgin olive oil
1½ tablespoon fresh rosemary, stems removed
2 teaspoons fresh thyme
¼ teaspoon smoked paprika
½ teaspoon fresh coarse ground black pepper
Kosher salt
Zest of 1 lemon
1 tablespoon of clarified butter


Method of Preparation:
1. Preheat oven to 350°.
2. Create a paste. Add garlic, salt, rosemary, thyme, pepper and paprika to a food processor. Pulse a few times.
3. Add olive oil and butter to processor and continue to pulse into a paste. Remove paste from processor and add lemon zest.
4. Rub the paste on both sides of the chops. Wrap in plastic wrap and marinate for 20 - 30 minutes in the refrigerator.
5. Remove from refrigerator and let chops come to room temperature.
6. Heat a grill pan on medium-high heat. Spray with non-stick cooking spray. Add the chops and sear for about 3 minutes on each side.
7. Place seared chops in a 350° degree preheated oven for 2 to 4 minutes or until done .
8. Lamb chops are best served medium rare.

# Soups

Monday's Soup 20

Just-in-Thyme Split Pea Soup 21

Congee 23

Curry Chicken Noodle Soup 24

Twisted Italian Soup or "Soup Just Happens" 26

Shrimp Pho 28

Coconut & Ginger Butternut Squash Soup 30

White Bean, Kale and Sausage Soup 32

Crispy Flavored Bread Crumbs 32

Chilled Strawberry Soup (Gazpacho) 34

Chilled Pea Soup with Seared Salmon 36

Kimchi & Seafood Soup 37

Mulligatawny Soup 40

# Monday's Soup

4 slices of bacon, diced
1/2 cup onions, diced
1/2 cup celery, diced
1/2 cup carrots, diced
1/2 tsp. kosher salt
Pinch fresh ground pepper
1/2 teaspoon smoky paprika
1/2 cup tomatoes, diced
2 teaspoons garlic, minced
8 cups chicken stock
1 cup beef stock

1 tablespoon tomato paste
1/2 teaspoon hot sauce
1 dried bay leaf
1/4 teaspoon fresh sage, finely chopped
2 teaspoons fresh thyme, finely chopped
1 ½ cup fresh kale, chopped
2 cans butter beans, rinsed & drained
1 can pinto beans, rinsed & drained
Fresh made croutons, topping
Fresh scallions, topping

## Method of Preparation

1. Cook the bacon in a Dutch oven over medium high heat for approximately 3 minutes or until crispy. Remove and set aside on a paper towel lined plate.
2. Add the onions, celery and carrots to the bacon oil. Stir together and season with salt, pepper and paprika. Cook for approximately 5 minutes until the vegetables are tender and lightly caramelized.
3. Add the tomatoes and garlic. Gently stir for another 30 seconds.
4. Pour in the chicken and beef stocks, tomato paste and add hot sauce.
5. Stir all the ingredients together and allow the liquids to come to a boil. Once the liquids come to a boil, lower the temperature to a simmer and continue cooking for 25 to 35 minutes.
6. Add the bay leaf, sage, thyme, kale, butter beans and pinto beans to the pot.
7. Stir the ingredients together and continue cooking at a simmer for another 15 to 20 minutes or until the beans are heated through and the kale is tender.
8. Garnish with croutons and scallions.

# Just-in-Thyme Split Pea Soup

## Ingredients

4 tablespoons of olive oil
2 carrots, medium dice
3 onions, medium dice, divided (2 for soup,
1 for mushrooms)
3 stalks of celery, chopped
2 cups split peas
2 tablespoons fresh parsley
1 tablespoon fresh cilantro, chopped
4 cloves of roasted garlic, smashed

8 cups vegetable stock
Kosher salt
Fresh ground black pepper

## Ingredients for the topping

1 lb. button mushrooms
3 teaspoons fresh thyme, chopped
¼ cup dry white wine
8 tablespoons grated Parmesan
½ cup heavy cream, plus extra for garnish

## Method of Preparation

1. In a large pot or Dutch oven, heat 2 tablespoons of olive oil. Add carrots, 2 diced onions, and celery. Cook until vegetables are soft and tender, approximately 6 or 7 minutes.
2. Add the split peas, parsley, cilantro, smashed garlic and stock. Cover and bring to a boil. Reduce heat to simmer for 45 minutes or until the peas are tender. Add salt and pepper to taste, stir and keep on warm.
3. In a sauce pan, add the remaining oil. Allow to heat. Add the remaining diced onion and cook for 3 minutes or until translucent. Add the mushrooms, thyme, salt and pepper. Cover and allow the mushrooms to release their juices. This will take about 2 to 3 minutes. Remove the lid and let the juices evaporate. This will give the mushrooms a golden glaze.
4. Next, add the wine to the mushrooms and allow it to evaporate. This will give the mushrooms a great flavor. Once the wine has evaporated, turn heat off.
5. For the soup, turn the heat up slightly and in small amounts add half of the mushroom mixture along with half of the parmesan cheese and a drizzle of the heavy cream. Stir to combine and serve.
6. Use the remaining mushrooms, cheese and heavy cream for garnishing.
Optional toppings are sour cream, bacon and parsley or a combination of all.

# Congee

Ingredients

For the Grits (Congee)
1 cup of Grits
4 to 5 cups of Chicken Stock (plus extra if needed)
¼ cup fresh ginger, divided (1/2 chunk, remaining chopped)
Kosher salt
Fresh ground black peppers
4 scallions, bottoms only (reserve greens for topping)
1 small onion, diced

For the Toppings
½ cup coconut oil (or your favorite oil)
4 cloves of garlic, chopped with a pinch of salt
Sweet Chinese sausage, sliced

Chorizo, sliced
Cherry tomatoes, halved, roasted
Sweet peppers, julienned, roasted
1 bunch of breech mushrooms, bottoms removed
¼ cup fresh parsley chopped
½ cup fresh cilantro, whole leaves, stems removed
1 bunch (or 12 ounces) Chinese broccoli, cut
Optional: Red pepper flakes can be added to broccoli when boiling for a little heat!

Twisted Oyster Sauce
1 tablespoon garlic infused oil
1 tablespoon Sesame Oil
3 tablespoons Oyster sauce
3 tablespoons hot chicken stock

## Method of Preparation:

1. In a large pot add chicken stock, chunk ginger, salt, scallion bottoms and onions, bring to a boil. Boil for 3 minutes then remove chunk vegetables and reduce heat slightly.
2. Whisk in the grits be careful to avoid burning yourself. Continue whisking, the grits begin to thicken. Reduce to a simmer and place a lid on the pot. Cook until done. Stir frequently.
3. In a large pan heat coconut oil. Add garlic stirring frequently until lightly browned. Remove garlic immediately to a paper towel lined plate. Garlic will crisp while sitting. Set aside.
4. In the same pan, add chorizo and cook until crisp. Remove chorizo to a lined baking sheet. Repeat the same process with the sweet sausage. Remove to baking sheet also. By following this process, you are seasoning the coconut oil with the garlic, chorizo and sweet sausage flavors...yum!
5. Next, add mushrooms to the pan. Cook until golden brown. Then add parsley and continue cooking for 2 minutes. Remove to the baking sheet. Reserve oil.
6. In a separate pot, bring salted water to a slight boil. If using red pepper flakes, add them to the pot. Add broccoli and cook for 3 to 5 minutes until slightly tender. Remove and drain very well. Set aside.
7. To make sauce: In a bowl, add 3 tablespoons of the reserved oil, add sesame oil and oyster sauce, whisk. Mixture will thicken. Add hot chicken stock and continue to whisk. Set sauce aside.
8. Place a serving of grits in a bowl and top with broccoli and sauce. Next add chorizo, sausage, tomatoes, peppers, ginger, crispy garlic and fresh cilantro.

# Curry Chicken Noodle Soup

Ingredients

2 tablespoons olive oil
1 cup onion, diced
½ cup celery, diced
½ cup red bell pepper, diced
½ cup yellow bell pepper, diced
3 tablespoons fresh ginger, minced
2½ tablespoons curry powder
2 teaspoons turmeric
7 cups chicken broth
3 tablespoons roasted garlic, smashed
1 small carrot, bias cut
½ cup fresh cilantro, divided
(half chopped, half whole)
1 very ripe banana, mashed
1 - 8oz package pasta noodles
1/3 cup coconut milk

Kosher salt
Fresh ground pepper
1 ½ cups chicken, cooked, shredded and warm
1 zucchini, cut half-moon and browned on the stove
Water as needed
Bunch of Thai basil

Additional topping choices
Fresh spinach, chopped
Fresh cilantro, chopped
Fresh Shaved Parmesan
Lime wedges

Method of Preparation:

1. Heat oil in a large pot or Dutch oven sauté onions, celery, bell peppers and ginger. Cook for 5minutes.
2. Add the curry powder and turmeric and continue cooking for another 3 minutes.
3. Add the broth, smashed garlic, carrot, chopped cilantro and banana. Stir to incorporate. Cover and bring to a slight boil.
4. When ready to serve, add the noodles and continue cooking for another 8 minutes (or until the pasta is al dente).
5. Pour in the coconut milk, chicken, zucchini and season with salt and pepper. Bring up to temperature.
6. Ladle into a bowl and top with basil, cilantro, spinach or parmesan and a lime wedge.

# Twisted Italian Soup or "Soup Just Happens"

I don't know about you, but I love a good, stick-to-my-tummy soup on a brisk fall or cold winter day. Add a nice glass of wine and you won't see me until the next morning! Here's a soup I made one day for my family while I was developing a new, whole grain, cornmeal cornbread recipe (but please, use your favorite cornbread recipe).

For this recipe, I started by browning some Italian sausage, both hot and sweet. I then drained the meat and set it aside. Next, I drizzled a little oil in the pot and added my onions and garlic. Once the onions were translucent I added chunk, fresh rutabagas, diced carrots, and half of a sweet potato which I diced also. I browned the root vegetables for about 5 to 7 minutes and then added my broth using enough to cover the vegetables.

I cooked this for about 10 minutes to allow the flavors to harmonize. Next, I added fresh, chopped thyme, dried parsley, turmeric, a variety of canned, rinsed beans and peas (cannellini, chick peas, black-eyed peas) and a can of whole, peeled tomatoes. I used my potato masher to smash a few of the beans, peas and tomatoes. Doing this will act as a thickener without having to add flour or cornstarch, but if you feel better using either, please do so.

I returned the meat to the pot and added a little more broth to cover all the ingredients. Lastly, I covered the pot with a tight-fitting lid and allowed the soup to cook until the beans and peas were tender and my desired flavor had been reached. In the last 5 minutes of cooking, I added sea salt, fresh ground black pepper and chopped, fresh kale.

An optional small amount of heavy cream at this point may be added to the pot for a richer soup. I served it over a slice of my new cornmeal cornbread and shared some with my neighbors! I needed the feedback.

For this soup, I really did not measure the ingredients because I make it slightly different each time (trying out a new herb, adding tomato sauce instead of tomatoes, adding potatoes...it just depends). Try it out and use as much or as little of any ingredient you choose.

Send me feedback at simplychefrenee@gmail.com. I'd love to hear from you.

# Shrimp Pho

## Ingredients
1 package rice noodles, cooked

### Broth
Vegetable oil
1 onion, chopped
1-2 celery stalks
1 fennel bulb, halved
6 scallions, bias chopped, divided
1 jalapeno, sliced (seeds removed for less heat),
2 tablespoons fresh ginger, thinly sliced
32 oz. chicken stock
2½ tablespoon miso paste
½ bunch bok choy, bottom only, chopped
(reserve tops)

## Ingredients for cooked toppings
2 tablespoons butter, divided
2 tablespoons sesame oil
½ bunch of bok choy, tops and bottoms chopped
12 shrimps, peeled, deveined
8 oz. baby bella mushrooms, quartered, stems removed
¼ cup hoisin sauce
3 tablespoons soy sauce
Kosher salt
Fresh ground black pepper

### Fresh Toppings
2 bunches of fresh basil (whole and Thai)
2 sprigs of fresh mint
2 carrots, peeled and julienned
12 oz. bean sprouts
½ bulb fennel, thinly sliced
Fresh cilantro (1 bunch)
1 lime, cut into wedges

## Method of Preparation
1. Cook noodles according to package instructions, set aside. (Reheat at service time.)
2. In a large stock pot heat vegetable oil. Add onions. Cook over medium temperature just to slightly caramelize.
3. Add celery, ½ fennel, 2 scallions, jalapeno and ginger. Cook until aromatic. Add stock and miso paste and bring to a simmer. Continue cooking until fully flavored for 30-40 minutes.
4. Using a slotted spoon, remove all the ingredients from broth and keep the broth covered and warming. Add salt and pepper to taste. Keeping the broth hot is necessary for this dish.
5. In a separate large sauté pan, add butter and sesame oil. When hot, add white chunk bottoms of bok choy and sauté until slightly translucent. Remove and set aside.
6. Add a little more oil (if necessary) and sauté the shrimp on both sides. Remove and set aside.
7. To the same pot, add the mushrooms and cook for 2 to 3 minutes. Add hoisin sauce to coat mushrooms. Add salt and pepper to taste then remove and set aside.
8. To serve: Reheat the noodles.
9. Place a serving of noodles in the center of each large bowl. Ladle broth generously into each bowl.
10. Pile bean sprouts on top of the noodles. Then surround the sprouts with shaved fennel, fresh carrots, bok choy greens and cooked bottoms. Add mushrooms and shrimp.
11. Top with jalapeno slices and fresh cilantro.
12. Serve immediately with a side plate containing lime wedges, fresh basil, fresh mint leaves and more sprouts. Side sauces are chili paste and soy sauce.

# Coconut & Ginger Butternut Squash Soup

## Ingredients

1 large butternut squash, peeled, large dice
1 sweet potato, peeled, large dice
Garlic infused olive oil
Kosher salt
3 tablespoons butter
2 teaspoons fresh ginger, minced
1 large onion, large dice
1 fennel bulb, diced
4 ½ cups chicken stock
1 (15oz) can coconut water

Pinch of cayenne pepper
1 (14 oz.) can unsweetened coconut milk
1 tablespoon fresh squeezed lemon juice

Toasted Walnut Cream (topping)
1 cup walnuts, toasted
¾ cup heavy cream chilled
¼ teaspoon hazelnut extract

## Method of Preparation:

1.  Place squash and sweet potato chunks on a parchment lined baking sheet. Drizzle with oil and sprinkle with salt. Roast in the oven until very tender. Remove and allow to cool.
2.  In a large Dutch oven add butter, ginger, onions and fennel. Cook until the onions and fennel are soft. Next, add the sweet potato, squash, chicken stock, coconut water and a pinch of cayenne pepper. Cover and cook for about 15 to 20 minutes. Test the potatoes and squash they should be soft and falling apart.
3.  Off heat, add the coconut milk to the pot and stir. Leave off heat.
4.  Puree squash in blender in batches (or use an immersion blender) until smooth. Using a sieve and a rubber spatula, pour puree into a large container. Add lemon juice, stir and taste.

## Toasted Walnut Cream

In a food processor, grind walnuts until very fine. Set aside.
In a separate, chilled metal bowl, beat heavy cream and hazelnut extract until soft peaks form.
Fold ¾ of the ground walnuts into the cream. Add a little salt if desired, fold again and set aside.

## To Serve:

Ladle soup into a bowl and add a small dollop of the Toasted Walnut Cream and a sprinkle of the remaining walnuts with a pinch of smoked paprika.

# White Bean, Kale and Sausage Soup

Ingredients

2 slices bacon, crisp, crumbled
8 ounces sweet Italian sausage (casings removed)
4 ounces hot sausage
1 small red onion, chopped
1 small white onion, chopped
1 celery stalk, diced
6 garlic cloves, minced
1 15-ounce can of cannellini beans, drained and rinsed
1 can great northern beans

1 can tomatoes, peeled, diced
6 cups chicken broth
¼ cup heavy cream (optional)
2 cups fresh kale, stems removed, chopped
Kosher salt
Fresh ground pepper
1 tablespoons fresh cilantro, rough chopped
Parmesan cheese, shaved

Method of Preparation

1. In a large pot, cook bacon until crisp. Remove from drippings, crumble and set aside.
2. Add the sausage to the bacon drippings and cook until browned.
3. Add onions, celery and garlic and continue cooking until onions are slightly translucent.
4. Add the beans, chicken broth and tomatoes. Bring to a boil. Reduce heat and cook for 30 minutes.
5. Optional: Add the heavy cream stirring to incorporate. And cook on low for another 10 minutes or until the beans are tender. If NOT using heavy cream continue to step 6.
6. Add the kale and cook for another 15 minutes.
7. Add salt and pepper to taste.
8. Garnish with fresh cilantro, bacon crisps or parmesan shavings.

# Crispy Flavored Bread Crumbs for Soup

Ingredients

½ Panko bread crumbs (plain)
2 tablespoons clarified butter
Fresh sage, very finely chopped
Pinch of cayenne
Kosher salt, pinch
Fresh ground pepper

Method of preparation

1. Preheat oven to 350°-375°. Line a baking sheet with parchment paper. Set aside.
2. Mix all ingredients in a bowl until coated and crumbly.
3. Spread crumbs on lined baking sheet being sure no clumps or lumps appear.
4. Place baking sheet in oven and bake until golden brown and crispy.

# Chilled Strawberry Soup (Gazpacho)

*Read the entire recipe prior to starting this soup. This soup will take a little while but I promise it is well worth the wait!*

## Ingredients

1½ pounds of fresh strawberries, divided
(1 lb. halved and hulled; ½ lb. diced)
4 additional strawberries, tops removed,
sliced top to bottom
½ peach, peeled and cut
1 large tomato, chopped
½ English cucumber, peeled and cut
1 large red bell pepper, seeded and cut
2 garlic cloves, roasted
2 sprigs of fresh thyme, chopped
Garlic infused extra virgin olive oil

¾ cup vegetable stock
1 tablespoon of Peach & White Balsamic
Vinegar (or just balsamic vinegar)
Kosher salt, to taste
Fresh ground pepper, to taste

For the topping:
Mix the diced strawberries (sparingly)
with a Garlic & Truffle Infused Olive oil.

## Method of Preparation

1. In a food processor, pulse tomato, cucumber and bell pepper until finely chopped. Pour into a bowl and set aside.
2. Add 1 pound of strawberries to the food processor and chop until fine. Pour into the tomato mixture. Stir and divide into 3 parts. Set one part aside to add at the end.
3. This next part you will need to do in 2 batches.
4. Of the 2 remaining batches, add 1 into the food processor. Add half of the garlic and half of the fresh thyme. Process until almost smooth. Remove to a fresh bowl. Repeat with remaining batch. When complete, pour the batches together (batches 2 and 3).
5. Add salt, pepper, vinegar and olive oil to the bowl. Taste.
6. Optional: If you want a smoother texture, strain using a sieve.
7. Add diced strawberries and stir.
8. Optional and recommended: Adjust texture and taste using the remaining third of mixture. Add salt and pepper as needed or desired.
9. Chill soup for at least 2 hours. When ready for service, remove from refrigerator and stir in the broth. Taste. Adjust seasonings as desired.
10. Garnish with sliced (or diced) strawberries and fresh thyme leaves. Drizzle with a little Peach White Balsamic Oil or Truffle Oil.

*Notes:*
*Peel the cucumber as the skins will change the taste of the soup.*
*I roasted my garlic and used fresh vegetable stock, but store bought will do fine.*
*I sautéed half of my bell pepper for added flavor.*
*Keep fresh chopped tomatoes and strawberry puree in the event you need to thicken the soup or additional flavoring is desired.*
*Peach Balsamic Vinaigrette and Truffle Oil are available in many stores.*

# Chilled Pea Soup with Seared Salmon

### Ingredients
4 quarts water
1 onion, quartered
3 garlic cloves, smashed
½ teaspoon turmeric
2 cups frozen peas
15 oz. vegetable broth
Juice of 1 lemon
¼ cup garlic infused olive oil
Pinch of white pepper
Salt, to taste
Toasted bread crumbs

### Seared Salmon
4 – 6 oz. Salmon, cut into single-serve pieces
Juice of ½ lemon
½ teaspoon hot paprika
¼ teaspoon fresh ground pepper
¼ teaspoon garlic powder
Chili paste, to taste
10 mint leaves, chopped
1 teaspoon coarse salt
Pinch of brown sugar
Olive oil

### Method of Preparation
1. In a large pot add water, onion, garlic and turmeric. Bring to a boil.
2. Using a strainer, remove the onion and garlic and dispose of them. Add the peas to the boiling water and blanch for 1 to 2 minutes (or until vibrant green). Remove immediately.
3. In a blender, add peas, broth (which will cool the peas down), lemon juice and a pinch of pepper. Blend until smooth. Slowly add in the olive oil and continue to blend.
4. Remove from blender to a container and add salt to taste. Place in the refrigerator to cool completely.
5. For the salmon, preheat oven to 375°F. Mix paprika, pepper, garlic powder, salt and brown sugar together in a small bowl. Set aside.
6. On a parchment or foil-lined baking sheet, add salmon pieces.
7. Pour ½ of the lemon juice over salmon. Drizzle with olive oil. Sprinkle with seasonings.
8. Using a heavy-bottomed pan heat on medium-high. Drizzle pan with oil.
9. Place salmon pieces, seasoned side down in pan. Sear until dark. Turn salmon over and place entire pan into the oven to finish salmon.
10. Cook until the salmon is pink all around (about 5 or so minutes).
11. Remove from the oven and allow to rest until completely cooled.
12. In the meantime, add remaining lemon juice, mint and chili paste to a bowl. Mix.
13. When salmon is cooled, flake and add to lemon juice mixture. You will have extra salmon so feel free to be generous or use for another dish. Season with salt and pepper if desired.

### To serve:
Remove the soup from the refrigerator and stir. Pour a serving into a container and top with a handful of the salmon mixture. Sprinkle with toasted bread crumbs and serve. Proper cooking temperature for salmon is 145°F.

To toast bread crumbs: Melt 2 tablespoons of butter in a bowl. Add bread crumbs to bowl and mix until coated. Spread on a baking sheet and place in a 400° preheated oven and bake until crispy and browned. (Oil can be substituted for butter.)

# Kimchi & Seafood Soup

## Ingredients

1½ tablespoon of garlic infused olive oil
½ tablespoon of sesame oil
3 ounces fresh breech mushrooms (or your favorite mushroom)
½ small onion, diced
2 scallions, divided (bottoms and tops) bias cut
1 celery stalk, diced
2 cloves garlic, crushed and chopped
1 tablespoon fresh ginger, finely chopped
2 quarts of seafood stock
½ cup dry white wine
2 tablespoons fresh cilantro, chopped
1 teaspoon turmeric
1 bunch of bok choy, green parts only, chopped
1 pound cod, cut into chunks
1 pound of shrimp, deveined, shells and tails removed
3 tablespoons miso paste
2 cups kimchi cabbage, drained and chopped

## Method of Preparation

1. In a large Dutch oven add both oils and heat on medium-high. Add mushrooms and onions and cook until the mushrooms turn brown.
2. Add the garlic, ginger, celery and scallion bottoms. Cook for another 3 minutes or until fragrant.
3. Pour in the stock, wine and sprinkle with turmeric. Bring to a boil uncovered.
4. Add the bok choy and cilantro and continue cooking for another 4 minutes.
5. Reduce heat slightly and add fish and shrimp. Cover and cook until the fish is done.
6. Remove the pot from the stove to prevent over cooking the seafood.
7. In a separate bowl, add the kimchi and miso. Stir. Using kitchen shears cut the kimchi into smaller bite – sized pieces.
8. Very carefully and gently, add the kimchi mixture to the soup trying to avoid breaking up the fish.
9. Garnish with scallions or cilantro and serve.

# Mulligatawny Soup

Ingredients

1 tablespoon butter (ghee)
1 tablespoon infused extra virgin olive oil
5 cloves garlic, chopped
1 large white onion, chopped
1 carrot, diced
1 celery stalk, diced
2 bay leaves
½ teaspoon each, cayenne pepper,
turmeric, cumin
2 teaspoons garam masala

1 tablespoon curry
1¾ teaspoon ground coriander
1/8 teaspoon ginger minced
2 cups red lentils
8 cups chicken stock
2 Granny Smith apples, diced (in lemon water)
1 14-oz. can of unsweetened coconut milk
Zest and juice of 1 lemon
1 lime, juiced
Fresh Cilantro, chopped

Method of Preparation

1. In a large, heavy pot set to medium heat, add oil and butter. When the butter is melted add the onions, carrots and celery cook until the onions are translucent. Add garlic and continue to cook for another minute.
2. Add half of the diced apples to the pot (reserve the remainder for garnish). Continue to cook and stir until the apple blends in and begins to break down.
3. Next, add the spices (red pepper flakes, paprika, cayenne pepper, turmeric, garam masala, coriander and cumin). Cook for another 2 minutes before adding the stock.
4. Add the stock and stir scraping the sides and bottom. Next, add the lentils, bay leaves and ginger. Bring to a boil. Reduce heat, cover and cook for about 25 minutes.
5. Remove 1/3 of the thickened soup mixture and set aside. Remove and discard the bay leaves. Using the immersion blender, blend the removed soup.
6. Return the blended soup to the pot and add the coconut milk, lemon zest and lemon juice. Stir. Season with salt and pepper.
7. Mix the remaining apples with a bunch of chopped cilantro and ½ of lime juice. Season with salt and pepper to taste.
8. To serve. Place a serving of the soup into a bowl and top with the apple/cilantro mixture. Enjoy!

# Salads

The Wedge Salad 43

Salmon with Warmed Rainbow Vegetable Salad 46

Spinach, Sweet Potato & Apple Salad 48

Haricot Vert & Pear Tomato Salad 50

Caesar Salad 52

Sugar Snap Pea & Chicken Salad 54

Colorful Couscous Salad 55

Figs, Greens & Stuffed Salmon Salad 58

Cabbage, Kale & Carrots 60

Renée's Panzanella Salad 61

# The Wedge Salad

Ingredients
1 cup of cherry or grape tomatoes, halved or quartered
1 cup of blue cheese crumbled, divided
1 head of iceberg lettuce, rinsed, cut into wedges
Kosher salt
Fresh ground black pepper
1 cup of buttermilk dressing
4 slices of bacon
Small bunch of fresh chives, snipped

Method of Preparation
1. Cook bacon. Crumble and set aside.
2. Place several wedges of lettuce onto a serving platter.
3. Top each wedge with equal amounts of Blue Cheese Buttermilk Dressing (see index) allowing it to run down the sides.
4. Sprinkle with blue cheese crumbles using the dressing as glue.
5. Top with cut tomatoes and bacon.
6. Grind black pepper directly on top of salad. Add salt if desired.
7. Sprinkle with chives and serve with a side of Blue Cheese Buttermilk Dressing.

Note: Grilled shrimp, chicken or steak can be substituted for the bacon (or keep the bacon too!).

# Salmon with Warmed Rainbow Vegetable Salad

*In recognition of Osteoporosis Month: "A Salad Promoting Healthy Bones!"*
*When developing this recipe I tried to make choices that would serve our bones best while continu-*
*ing to create a flavorful dish. With that said, I used extra virgin olive oil because it contains the most*
*polyphenols and is the least processed of olive oils. The polyphenols have natural alkalizing properties*
*and are bone smart. Here's to bones!*

Ingredients

2 cups each kale, red cabbage, bok choy, broccoli and romaine lettuce
1 small sweet potato, diced
2 tablespoons fresh parsley leaves
Pumpkin seeds, garnish
Almonds sliced, optional garnish
Sunflower seeds, optional garnish
Kosher Salt
Fresh ground black pepper to taste
Cognac Prune Dressing (see index)
Extra Virgin Olive Oil

Method of Preparation

1. Drizzle a little oil in a large pan. Sauté the bok choy and remove to a bowl.
2. Sauté kale and broccoli with a pinch of salt and parsley. Add to the bowl of bok choy.
3. Drizzle a little oil to the pan and add the sweet potatoes and a little water (to steam the potatoes) and allow it to evaporate leaving a light sear. Add potatoes to the mixture.
4. Drizzle a little more oil to the pan and add the red cabbage and a pinch of salt and pepper.
5. Add a dressing (your favorite or the Cognac Prune Dressing) to the pan; continue to sauté the cabbage for another minute. Garnish with sliced almonds, pumpkin seeds and/or sunflower seeds.
6. Remove from heat. Toss the cabbage with vegitable mix. Add the fresh, crisp romaine and toss again.
7. To serve: Add a serving of the salad to the plate. Top with salmon and garnish.

# Seared Salmon

Ingredients

4 -6 2.5 oz. cuts of Wild Salmon
Chipotle paprika seasoning
Pinch of kosher salt
1 tablespoon garlic infused olive oil
¼ teaspoon lemon pepper, optional

Method of Preparation

Season the salmon. Rub the seasoned fish with oil. Heat a heavy bottom skillet on medium-high heat. Drizzle with a little oil. Sear the salmon for about 3 minutes on the first side, turn it over and cook for another 2 to 3 minutes. (If the fish is thin cook time is less.) Proper cooking temperature for fish is 145°F.

# Spinach, Sweet Potato & Apple Salad

Ingredients
2 cups fresh baby spinach
½ cup mixed greens
1 sweet potato, diced
1 small red onion, diced
1 small Granny Smith Apples, julienned
1 boiled egg, diced
2 tablespoons pomegranate seeds
Champagne vinaigrette (or your favorite vinaigrette)
Fresh ground black pepper
Optional: toasted walnuts

Method of Preparation
1. Preheat oven to 400° and line a baking sheet with parchment paper.
2. In a bowl add the potato and red onion. Drizzle with a little oil and season with salt and pepper. Bake in oven until potatoes are tender. Remove and allow to cool.
3. Cut apple into thin strips and place in cold water with 2 slices of lemon until ready to use.
4. For service: Add a little of your favorite dressing to the mixed greens and spinach. Toss with your hand and place on serving plate.
5. Sprinkle a few potato and red onions on top.
6. Add the egg, apple strips, pomegranate seeds and nuts.
7. Top with fresh ground black pepper and enjoy!

# Haricot Vert & Pear Tomato Salad

Ingredients

1 pound haricot vert, trimmed
1 pint yellow pear tomatoes, halved
1 tablespoon balsamic vinegar
1 tablespoon extra virgin olive oil
¼ teaspoon ground mustard
¼ teaspoon nutritional yeast flakes
1 teaspoon honey
1 pinch kosher salt

Method of Preparation

1.  In a pot of salted hot water, blanch haricot vert. Remove to a large bowl of iced water and "shock." Pat the haricot vert dry.
2.  Heat a large sauté pan. Do not add oil. Add the haricot vert and slightly char swirling beans around until done.
3.  In a bowl, whisk together the vinegar, mustard, yeast and honey. Slowly add oil while continuing to whisk to create an emulsion. Taste and set aside.
4.  Toss the charred haricot vert, tomatoes, salt and vinaigrette together in a large bowl. Serve.

*I developed this recipe during my years in culinary school which I enjoyed very much. It is colorful, tasty and good for you too! I hope you enjoy this easy to prepare salad which can be eaten warm or cold.*

# Caesar Salad

2 large egg yolks
6 anchovy fillets in oil
2 garlic cloves, roasted
¾ teaspoon dijon mustard
¼ cup mayonnaise
2 tablespoons fresh squeezed lemon juice
½ teaspoon Worcestershire sauce
2 tablespoons extra virgin olive oil
½ cup vegetable oil
3 tablespoons parmesan cheese, grated
Fresh ground black pepper
Fresh shaved parmesan cheese, topping

Method of Preparation
1. Whisk egg yolks in a large bowl.
2. Chop anchovy fillets on a cutting board. Smash with roasted garlic.
3. Add anchovy mix to the egg yolk and whisk together.
4. Add the mustard and mayonnaise and continue whisking.
5. Add lemon juice and Worcestershire sauce. Mix again.
6. Whisk in the oils until desired taste and consistency.
7. Stir in grated parmesan and black pepper.
8. Garnish with shaved parmesan.

Add-ons:
Garlic shrimp
Pinch of red pepper flakes
Pinch of cayenne pepper
Minced dried cranberries (for sweet)

# Sugar Snap Pea & Chicken Salad

½ lb. sugar snap peas
1½ cup chicken, cooked and torn into pieces
3 cups mixed greens
1 cup arugula
¼ cup dried cranberries
½ cup pecans, toasted (optional)
Pinch of seasoned salt
Fresh ground black pepper
Extra virgin olive oil
Berry Vinaigrette

## Method of Preparation

1. Blanch and shock snap peas. Drain, pat dry and set aside.
2. In a large sauté pan drizzle oil. Add peas and cook for about 1 minute or until nicely coated.
3. Add a pinch of seasoned salt and fresh ground pepper to taste. Place in a bowl and keep warm.
4. Add chicken to the pan. Heat until golden brown.
5. Mix chicken and snap peas.
6. To serve. Place mixed greens and arugula in a bowl and gently toss with Berry Vinaigrette.
7. Add a serving of the greens to a serving plate.
8. Sprinkle with cranberries and pecans.
9. Top with sugar snap peas and chicken.

# Colorful Couscous Salad

Tri-color Israeli Couscous
¼ cup sun-dried tomatoes, chopped
¼ cup black pitted olives, sliced
1 celery stalk, thin bias cut
¼ each bell peppers, red, yellow and orange, diced
½ English cucumbers, diced
1 lb. haricot vert
2 tablespoons fresh herbs (I used parsley and chives)
Kosher salt, to taste
Fresh ground black pepper, to taste
Pinch red pepper flakes, optional
Lemon-Honey Dijon Vinaigrette (see index)

## Method of Preparation

1. Cook couscous according to package directions. Place in a bowl and allow to cool.
2. In a large pot of salted water, blanch haricot vert. When vibrant green, about 1 to 2 minutes, remove to a large bowl of iced water. Drain and pat dry. Cut into bite-sized pieces. Set aside.
3. Add sun-dried tomatoes, olives, celery, bell peppers, cucumbers to a large bowl.
4. Add fresh herbs and cooled couscous and mix together.
5. Add dressing, salt and pepper to taste.
6. If using red pepper flakes, gently fold into salad and serve.

# Figs, Greens & Stuffed Salmon Salad
## (Celebration Salad created for the "We Can Cook" Event)

6 oz. red and green leaf lettuce, torn into pieces
4 oz. baby spinach
6 oz. baby kale
1 cup watercress
1 bunch asparagus, roasted, bite-sized
¼ red cabbage, cut to torn lettuce sizes
1 small jicama, julienned
8 to 10 oz. wild smoked sockeye salmon
¼ cup fennel, thinly sliced and chopped
4 oz. cream cheese, softened

2 tablespoons dill, chopped
1 tablespoon capers, chopped
1 teaspoon lemon juice
Fresh ground black pepper
Pomegranate seeds
4-6 figs, (fresh roasted or poached) cut into wedges
Champagne "Fizzy" Fig Dressing

Method of Preparation
1. In a large bowl mix all salad greens and set aside.
2. In a separate bowl, coat red cabbage, asparagus and jicama with a small amount of fig dressing. Set aside.
3. In another bowl add fennel, cream cheese, dill, capers and lemon juice. Stir until fully incorporated. Season with black pepper.
4. Lay thinned salmon pieces on a cutting board. Add 1 scoop of cream cheese mixture to the salmon. Roll salmon around cream cheese mixture and set aside until all rolls have been completed. Sit salmon rolls upright and garnish with sprinkles of dill on top until service. Set aside.
5. Using your hands, add red cabbage mixture greens and gently toss to coat with dressing.
6. Add a bunch of the salad mixture to a serving plate. Arrange wedges of figs and rolls of salmon around the salad (or to the side of the salad or on top).
7. Sprinkle the salad with pomegranate seeds and chives.
8. Serve with a side of Champagne "Fizzy" Fig Dressing.

# Champagne Fizzy Fig Dressing

Ingredients

4 tablespoons olive oil
1 teaspoon coriander
1 teaspoon dijon mustard
2 figs
½ lemon juice, plus extra
1 garlic clove, roasted

1 tablespoon Champagne vinegar
½ tablespoon honey
Kosher salt
Fresh ground black pepper
Champagne

Method of Preparation
1. Combine first 8 ingredients in a food processor.
2. Process until fully incorporated. Mixture will be thick and mildly lumpy.
3. Add salt and pepper to taste.
4. When ready for service, top off dressing with Champagne to desired consistency and whisk together.

# Cabbage, Kale & Carrots

*With this recipe, use any amount of the ingredients you would like. It's a very sturdy and flexible salad. Eating in color never tasted so good!*

## Ingredients

Red Cabbage, chopped
Napa Cabbage, chopped
Cucumber, sliced
Kale, stemmed, chopped
Carrots, julienned or shredded
Scallions, sliced (bias)
Sesame Seeds, toasted
Cranberries
Cilantro
Nuts (optional)

## Dressing Ingredients

½ cup Olive oil
1 tablespoon sesame oil
2 tablespoons honey, plus extra
¼ cup rice wine vinegar
1/3 cup soy sauce
¼ cup oyster sauce
1 ½ teaspoon ginger, minced
1 teaspoon garlic, minced
Pinch of black pepper

## Method of Preparation

1. Place all ingredients, except the nuts, into a large bowl. Toss and set aside.
2. For the dressing, add all the ingredients in a large bowl except the oils. Whisk together.
3. Slowly drizzle the oils into the bowl and whisk to emulsify. Taste.
4. Adjust seasonings to your desired taste.
5. Prior to service pour dressing over the salad and sprinkle with your favorite nuts and sesame seeds.

# Renée's Panzanella Salad

*This salad is very quick, easy, colorful, nutritious and delicious to boot! It is sure to be the hit of the backyard barbeque or summer outing. I love making my Panzanella Salad because it's so darn tasty. Who cares if it also good for me.*

## Ingredients

1 yellow bell pepper, large dice
1 red bell pepper, large dice
1 orange bell pepper, large dice
1 large purple onion, large cut
2 zucchinis, large dice
1 baguette, cut into cubes
¼ cup fresh parsley

3 tablespoons mixed herbs, thyme, dill and oregano
1 pint of cherry tomatoes, whole
Garlic infused extra virgin olive oil
2 tablespoons unsalted butter, melted
Kosher salt
Fresh ground black pepper
Pinch of red pepper flakes

## Method of Preparation

1. Preheat the oven to 400°. Line a baking sheet with parchment paper. Set aside.
2. In a large bowl whisk 2 tablespoons of the mixed herbs, olive oil, butter and red pepper flakes.
3. Add the baguette cubes and toss to coat all the pieces. Add more oil if needed.
4. Transfer to the baking sheet and bake for 8 to 10 minutes tossing once until crispy and golden brown.
5. To the bowl add the peppers, onion and zucchini and toss to coat.
6. Sprinkle with salt and pepper. Toss again.
7. Heat a grill pan to medium-high heat. Brush pan with olive oil. In batches, cook the vegetables until charred. Remove and keep warm until all vegetables are done.
8. Toss vegetables with fresh parsley and a squeeze of lemon juice.
9. Fold in halved tomatoes and adjust seasoning with salt and pepper.

Optional: Mix with your favorite vinaigrette. Serve with croutons and enjoy!

# Chef Renée's Food Mantra

Food does not make us thin or fat. It does not (and cannot) make us happy or sad (although some would disagree). Food is, simply put, nourishment for our bodies which in turn provides us with energy to do the things we need to do, the things we want to do and the things we like to do. Food is a supplier of energy enabling us to go and to be. Sounds simple? I hope so, because it is.

Some foods are natural and some foods, I use the term "food" loosely here, are unnatural. Nevertheless, and in both cases, food is colorful, it is flavorful and like people food is ever changing and evolving. For some, food can be a means of taking control of your life and/or your health. It can provide you with the opportunity to create, monitor, mold, develop and shape your unique, incredible and miraculous existence. Who are you? Who do you want to be or to become? Although it seems that these questions cannot be answered simply by eating a food, our intake of food and our food choices however, can lead to the answers we seek. Food provides energy. It provides sustenance that empowers us. It nourishes our physical bodies so that we can focus more and clearer on our spiritual and emotional bodies. Food sustains our lives and offers an opportunity for longevity to experience life and all it has to offer. Food is indeed a good and wonderful thing.

Which foods to eat and not to eat are very personal decisions and can even be spiritual for some. Therefore, I will not be presumptuous by telling you what you can and cannot eat. That is a decision you must make either alone or with the help of your physician (or dietitian or nutritionist); but what I can tell you is that no matter which foods you chose to consume, I can offer you recipes and ideas on how to prepare them so that you can maximize you nutrient and vitamin intake and be healthier.

YOU are uniquely created with a specific DNA make up which includes a blood type, a chemical collaboration and many other wonderful things; but for simplicity's sake I'll just point out one other thing, your metabolic rate. I mention this more for energy's sake than burning calories, although as we burn calories we gain energy for use.

Your metabolic rate is important like the many other properties and functions of your body (all working systematically, regularly, and always) to make and allow you to be YOU. Without food, it would all stop. Just stop. No blood or fluid flow, no pumping and beating, no inflating and deflating. No producing or multiplying, no renewing, no intake or excretions; nothing. YOU, the fearfully, wonderfully and miraculously made you would cease to exist. It's that simple. We, you and I, need food to survive.

Never skip meals. Especially if you think you are doing yourself (your body) a favor. Instead, choose wisely what you eat. Take time to enjoy what you eat. Slow down and listen to your body tell you what it needs, what it wants you to eat.

This is probably the hardest part of changing your diet especially if you have been on "go" for a long time. You must learn to stop. Stop and breathe before you select a meal, a dish, or a snack. Close your eyes just for a moment and think about how and what your body is saying. What is it feeling? Is it tired? Is it stressed? Is it happy? Is it frustrated? Is it slow? Learn why you are eating. There are more reasons than just hunger that we eat and select the foods we choose to consume.

Eat first to address your body's needs. Supply it first; then you can have what YOU want. This sounds easy enough, right? Well it isn't! That is until you've done it a few times and then it becomes as natural as waking up and smiling. I'm a big proponent of seasonal eating. That is eating the food that is harvested in the current season. The earth produces the things both it and you require each season. I think someone, somewhere out there thought and thinks a lot of us and must really love us to create such harmony. Our bodies were created from substances of the earth, so why wouldn't it change when the "earth" changes. This is normal. This is spiritual (for some). We must learn to readjust, stop, take a breath and listen (again). What is your body telling you it requires (this time, this season)? You would be amazed at how differently you feel when you eat a bowl of homemade soup when you are sick versus eating a bowl of the same soup when you are well or even when your body is cold and simply wants something warm to comfort it. Because our bodies have different requirements in the examples above it will take what it needs first, use it to reboot (reenergize) and then allow you to finish the rest as a bonus. The same occurs with every bite of food you consume. Food is always working something in your body whether it be for good or for not-so-good.

Therefore, if you should eat and find that you are still hungry, it simply means that your body did not get enough of what it needs and it is still waiting for you to supply it. Fresh ingredients contain the most vitamins and nutrients, so try to stay closest to a foods natural state. Your body will be satisfied sooner causing you to eat less (or at least feel full sooner). Understanding this very basic principal is the foundation of developing and maintaining a positive relationship with food.

My desire is for you to be a healthier and a better you by building a wonderful relationship with food so you can focus on the other things in your life and in the world that give it meaning like laughter and love!

# Entrées

Stuffed Chicken Thighs 67

Smothered Chicken 70

Fried Pork Chops 72

Cider Brined Pork Chops with Cherry Brow Butter 74

Crispy Fried Chicken 76

Rum & Cola Braised Short Ribs 78

Filet Mignon 80

Seared Salmon 82

Citrus Glazed Chicken 84

Arugula, Fennel & Pear Salad 86

Seared Swordfish 86

Shrimp & Langoustine Risotto 88

Vegetable, Cheese & Tomato Tart 90

Roasted Cauliflower & Quinoa Salad 91

# Stuffed Chicken Thighs

## Ingredients

4 chicken thighs, boneless, skinless, flattened
4 slices of prosciutto, sliced thinly
4 string cheeses, cut in half, vertically, then horizontally (creating 4 pieces)
¼ cup melted butter melted
½ cup garlic infused extra virgin olive oil
Handful of fresh chopped parsley
¼ teaspoon dried oregano
¼ teaspoon dried marjoram
8 oz. fresh baby spinach

## Method of Preparation

1. Place a heavy bottom skillet on the stove and set to medium-high heat.
2. Separate the prosciutto pieces. Set one piece of the string cheese inside the prosciutto and roll wrapping the cheese completely. Set aside and repeat until all 4 pieces are done.
3. In a small bowl, mix the melted butter, infused oil, fresh parsley and dried herbs.
4. Drizzle a little oil into the pan and sauté 2 tablespoons of chopped onions.
   Then add 3 ounces of spinach and cook lightly. Remove mixture and set aside.
5. Brush the inside of the flattened chicken with the butter/oil mixture.
6. Place the prosciutto rolled cheese stick inside the thigh and add a scoop of the spinach mixture. Use a toothpick and close the chicken wrap. Brush the outsides of the chicken with butter mixture. Repeat until all thighs are done.
7. Place chicken in the hot skillet. Brown on all sides turning to get a golden-brown sear. Place in a preheated oven at 375° and cook until chicken is done. Test with a cooking thermometer.
   (Proper cooking temperature for poultry is 165°).
8. Remove and tent with foil for at least 10 minutes.
9. Serve with Mushroom & Shallot Sauce (see index) or a sauce or gravy of your own.

# Smothered Chicken

## Ingredients

1 whole chicken, cut into 8+ pieces
1 ¾ cups buttermilk
Vegetable or peanut oil
2 teaspoons smoky paprika
1¼ tablespoon kosher salt
1 teaspoon ground dried thyme
¾ teaspoons fresh ground pepper
Zest of ¾ of a lemon

## Ingredients for gravy

1 onion, cut
1 bell pepper, cut
1 tablespoon butter
1 tablespoon oil
2¼ cup chicken broth
½ cup buttermilk
3 ½ cups of all-purpose flour
2 teaspoons baking powder
1 teaspoon ground dried parsley
¾ teaspoon garlic powder
½ teaspoon cayenne pepper
Juice of 1 lemon

## Method of Preparation

1. Place 1¾ cups buttermilk in a large zipper-sealed bag. Add a pinch of cayenne pepper, 1 teaspoon of salt and the juice of one lemon to the bag. Seal and squeeze ingredients together. Add the chicken pieces to the bag and allow to sit for about 10 minutes.
2. In a large bowl combine, paprika, baking powder, parsley, thyme, garlic powder, ½ teaspoon cayenne, lemon zest and black pepper. Whisk together.
3. Remove about 1/4 cup of the buttermilk from the bag and mix it into the flour ingredients thoroughly. The mix should be crumbly if not add more buttermilk from the bag.
4. Dredge each piece of chicken into the flour mixture and place on a rack atop a baking sheet.
5. When all of the chicken is floured, heat up a large Dutch oven with oil. The oil should not cover the chicken completely and the temperature of the oil should remain at approximately 360°- 375°. Add the chicken pieces to the pot without over crowding. Set ½ cup of seasoned flour aside for the gravy.
6. Cover with a lid and fry for about 4 or 5 minutes. Turn chicken pieces over and complete cooking for another 7 to 8 minutes. Chicken should be golden brown and the juices run clear. Remove to another clean rack lined baking sheet and allow to cool slightly.
7. In a separate large pot, add a drizzle of oil. Add the onions and bell peppers and cook. Add 1 tablespoon of butter and ¼ cup of the seasoned flour to the pot. Stir.
8. Add the chicken broth and whisk. This will prevent lumps from forming. Continue whisking until mixture begins to thicken. Stir in ½ cup of buttermilk.
9. Add the chicken to the gravy and cook for another 20 minutes or until the chicken is tender. Adjust seasoning as needed. If gravy too thick, loosen with water.
10. Serve over rice or mashed potatoes.

# Fried Pork Chops

6 pork chops
1½ cups all-purpose flour
1 cup of buttermilk
1 teaspoon kosher salt
¾ teaspoon fresh ground black pepper
½ teaspoon paprika
Pinch of cayenne pepper
1 tablespoon of ground dried parsley
Vegetable or peanut oil for frying

Method of Preparation
1. In a large bag combine flour, salt, ground black pepper, paprika and dried parsley. Close bag and shake seasonings together thoroughly. Set aside.
2. Pour buttermilk into a large bowl. Add the cayenne pepper and whisk.
3. Place the pork chops in the buttermilk and allow to sit for 10 to 15 minutes.
4. Remove the pork chops from the buttermilk and place into the flour mixture.
5. Shake off excess flour and place chops on a rack. Refrigerate.
6. When ready to cook, heat a heavy bottom pan (like a cast iron skillet) until the oil is very hot.
7. Fry the pork chops until done. Pork chops will be a beautiful golden brown color and crispy.

# Cider Brined Pork Chops with Cherry Brown Butter

## Ingredients

4-6 bone-in pork chops
(1½ inch thick)

### Brine
3 cups apple cider
4 cups ice cubes
Water (as needed)
1 onion, chopped
2 carrots, large dice
2 celery stalks, large dice
2 bay leaves
2 thyme sprigs
¾ teaspoon juniper berries
¾ teaspoon mixed peppercorns, whole
1 head garlic, halved horizontally

½ cup light brown sugar
½ cup kosher salt

### Cherry Brown Butter
3 tablespoons extra virgin olive oil
½ stick of butter
¼ cup dried cherries
2 sprigs fresh thyme
Kosher salt
Fresh ground black pepper

## Method of Preparation
1. Place the onions, celery, carrots, sugar, salt, garlic, peppercorns and bay leaves into a large pot. Heat on medium and stir until all the salt and sugar is dissolved. This will create a small liquid in the bottom of the pot. Once the liquid appears turn the burner off.
2. Add the fresh thyme, room temperature cider and the room temperature water. Stir to combine.
3. Using a very large bowl, add the ice and then pour the brine over the ice and stir. This should cool the brine down significantly. The brine must be cooled completely.
4. Place pork in the brine. Cover and refrigerate for a minimum of 2 hours but up to 24 hours.
5. When ready to cook, remove the chops from the refrigerator and brine. Pat dry with paper towels.
6. Heat a heavy bottom pan such as a cast iron skillet. Drizzle with oil. Place 2 chops in the pan and cook until caramelized. Turn the chops over. Place the entire pan in a preheated 375°/400° oven to finish (about 4 to 6 minutes depending on the thickness of the chops).
7. For the Cherry Brown Butter. Using the same pan you cooked the pork chops in without washing it, add the butter. Allow to melt and bubble. Add in the fresh thyme sprigs and dried cherries. Stir to flavor and plump cherries. Add oil if desired. Return chops to the pan and baste continually until satisfied the chops are fully flavored. Serve immediately.

# Crispy Fried Chicken

1 whole chicken, cut up into 8+ pieces
1¾ cups buttermilk
Vegetable or peanut oil
3½ cups of all-purpose flour
2 teaspoons smoky paprika
2 teaspoons baking powder
1¼ tablespoon kosher salt
1 teaspoon ground dried parsley
1 teaspoon ground dried thyme
¾ teaspoon garlic powder

¾ teaspoons fresh ground black pepper
½ teaspoon cayenne pepper, plus extra
Zest of ¾ of a lemon
Juice of 1 lemon

## Method of Preparation

1. Place buttermilk in a large zipper-sealed bag. Add a pinch of cayenne pepper, 1 teaspoon of salt and the juice of one lemon to the bag. Seal and squeeze ingredients together. Add the chicken pieces to the bag and allow to sit for about 10 minutes.
2. In a large bowl combine, paprika, baking powder, parsley, thyme, garlic powder, ½ teaspoon cayenne, lemon zest, remaining salt and black pepper. Whisk together.
3. Remove 1/4 cup of the buttermilk from the bag and add to the flour ingredients. Mix together thoroughly. The mix should be crumbly if not add another ¼ cup.
4. Dredge each piece of chicken into the flour mixture and place on a rack atop a baking sheet.
5. When all the chicken is floured, heat up a large Dutch oven or cast-iron skillet with oil. The oil should not cover the chicken completely and the temperature of the oil should remain at approximately 360°-375°. Add the chicken pieces to the pot without ovecrowding.
6. Cover with a lid and fry for about 4 or 5 minutes. Turn chicken pieces over and complete the cooking for another 7 to 8 minutes. Chicken should be golden brown and the juices run clear. Remove to a clean rack and allow to cool slightly.

# Rum & Cola Braised Short Ribs

4 pound short ribs
4 tablespoons canola oil
2 onions, chopped
3 tablespoons garlic, minced
¼ cup all-purpose flour
½ teaspoon ground ginger
½ teaspoon onion powder
½ cup brown sugar

¾ cup dark rum
¼ cup soy sauce
1¾ cup of your favorite cola
½cup dried dark cherries
2 cups beef stock
Juice of 1 lemon
Sea salt
Fresh ground pepper
¼ teaspoon paprika

Method of Preparation

1. Preheat oven to 400°F.
2. Season short ribs with salt, pepper, onion powder and paprika. Set aside.
3. In a large Dutch oven, add oil and heat until hot.
4. Sear short ribs on all sides. Remove to a paper towel lined plate to drain.
5. To the Dutch oven, add onions and dried cherries. Cook until cherries are plump and onions are translucent. Add garlic and cook until fragrant.
6. Stir in flour and ginger.
7. Add stock, rum and cola. Cook for 5 minutes while whisking.
8. Add soy sauce, lemon juice and brown sugar, continue whisking until well incorporated and liquid starts to boil.
9. Return short ribs to the pot. Cover and place in preheated oven.
10. Reduce oven temperature to 350°F and cook for 2 ½ hours or until ribs are tender and a thick, dark, sticky sauce has formed. (It will thicken more as it sits.)
11. Remove from oven and allow to sit for at least 15 minutes.

I love serving this with cheesy, creamy polenta or as an appetizer so I can lick my fingers!
Don't tell anybody, Shhh!

# Filet Mignon
(Best Cooked Steak Ever!)

## Ingredients
2-8 ounce filets,
2½ tablespoons bourbon brown sugar seasonings
2 tablespoons cracked black pepper
1 tablespoon salt
¾ tablespoon smoked paprika
Pinch of garlic powder
Vegetable oil or Canola oil
Optional: Truffle Butter or Herb Butter

## Method of Preparation
1. Preheat oven to 400°.
2. Tie filet with kitchen twine around the sides to hold the shape. Mix all the seasonings together and massage into the steaks.
3. Wrap in plastic wrap and marinate. When ready to cook allow steak to come to room temperature.
4. Heat a cast iron skillet to medium-high heat. Drizzle a very small amount of oil into the pan.
5. Remove plastic wrap and place filet in a pan and sear. Cook 2 to 3 minutes on one side.
6. Turn steak over and cook for another 2 minutes. Place entire pan into the oven for approximately 7 minutes. Test temperature with a meat thermometer. Remove from oven when temperature reaches 125 degrees for medium rare. Proper cooking temperature for beef is 145 degrees (but you really don't want to spoil this cut).
7. Remove from oven and tent with foil and rest for 10 minutes. Residual heat will finish the cooking process.

Note: Although this steak requires NOTHING else. Feel free to top with truffle butter or an herb butter and enjoy!

# Seared Salmon

4-6 fillets 2.5 oz. Salmon
Chipotle paprika seasoning
Pinch of kosher salt
1 tablespoon garlic infused olive oil
¼ teaspoon lemon pepper, optional

Method of Preparation
1.  Season the salmon. Massage fish with oil.
2.  Heat a heavy bottom skillet to medium-high heat.
3.  Drizzle with a little oil. Sear the salmon for about 3 minutes.
    Turn it over and cook for another 2 to 3 minutes. (If the fish is thin cook time is less.)
4.  Proper cooking temperature for fish is 145°F.
5.  Rest fillets for 5 minutes. Serve.

# Citrus Glazed Chicken

Ingredients

Chicken & Vegetables

5 chicken legs
5 chicken thighs (bone-in)
5 or 6 baby potatoes or fingerlings
2 beets
1 red onion, cut into large chunks
3 tablespoons extra virgin olive oil
1 cup barley, uncooked
¼ cup golden raisins or dried apricots
Watercress for garnish
1 package of frozen peas
(edamame or another green)

Marinade Ingredients

1 lemon, large zest
Juice of 2 lemons
¼ cup fresh squeezed orange juice
1 tablespoon sugar
2 tablespoons honey
1 teaspoon salt
3 cloves garlic, quartered
1 tablespoon smoked paprika
½ teaspoon cayenne pepper

Method of Preparation

1. Preheat oven to 375°-400°F. Prepare the marinade. Add the zest, lemon juice, orange juice, sugar, honey, salt, garlic, paprika, cayenne and oil to a large bowl and mix together. Add ½ of the marinade and chicken pieces to a sealed zipperseal bag. Marinade for 3 hours to overnight.
2. Reserve the other half of the marinade.
3. When ready to cook remove chicken from the refrigerator and the bag and let it come to room tempreature.
4. In a large roasting pan with high sides (about 1 ½ to 2 inches) add the onion wedges and potatoes. Drizzle olive oil over the vegetables. Add salt, pepper and fresh rosemary sprigs to the pan. Place chicken on top of the vegetables. Add fresh ground pepper and a little oil Place in the preheated oven uncovered and cook for 30 minutes. Check in and baste as needed.
5. With the remaining marinade, pour into a small pot and cook the marinade down until slightly thick. After the chicken has cooked for 30 minutes, pour the thickened sauce on top and return to oven to cook until nicely browned.
6. Roast the beets about 40 minutes. Lay out 2 pieces of aluminum foil (to wrap each beet in). Place 1 beet on each piece. Drizzle olive oil on the beets and add salt and pepper. Roll beet in oil. Close the foil sealing each end but leaving space for steam. Cook until tender when donecarefully remove the skins and the root piece. Cut into quarters. Set aside.
7. Cook barley according to package directions. Add raisins and bring to a boil. Continue with directions.
8. When the chicken is done, scoop out most of the pan juices and ladle it into a sauce pan. Add the second bowl of marinade and allow to cook down by half. This is your topping. Set aside.
9. Steam your peas and set aside. Chop fresh herbs and set aside.
10. To assemble the plate, add barley, place chicken atop and add potatoes, onions, beets and peas around the chicken. Sprinkle with watercress and enjoy!

# Seared Swordfish

Ingredients
Ingredients
3 - 4 swordfish steaks (1 to 1¼ inch thick)
2 cloves garlic, minced
1 tablespoon dijon mustard
1-2 teaspoons fresh thyme, chopped
1 teaspoon fresh ginger, grated
¼ cup extra virgin olive oil
Zest of 1 lemon
Juice of ½ lemon
Kosher salt
Fresh ground black pepper

Method of Preparation
1. Make the marinade. Add the thyme, ginger, garlic, lemon juice, lemon zest, olive oil and dijon mustard to a large bowl and whisk.
2. Pour marinade over the fish and allow to sit for at least 15 minutes.
3. Heat a heavy-bottom grill pan. Brush with oil and cook swordfish.
4. Cook for 3 minutes on each side. Remove from burner and cover to rest.
5. Serve with a delicious salad. (See Arugula, Fennel & Pear Salad )

# Arugula, Fennel & Pear Salad

Ingredients
8 ounces arugula
1 medium pear, sliced
1 tomato, cut into wedges
½ bulb fennel, thinly sliced
8 ounces black olives, whole, pitted
Honey Vinaigrette (see index)

Method of Preparation
1. Place the thinly sliced fennel in a small bowl with white wine (or water) to soften. Set aside.
2. Place arugula in a bowl. Add fennel, pear, olives and a small amount of dressing to the bowl and toss.
3. Garnish with seasoned tomatoes. Serve.

# Shrimp & Langoustine Risotto

## Ingredients

½ pound shrimp, peeled and deveined
½ pound langoustine, peeled and cooked
4½ cups seafood broth
2½ cups water
2 cups arborio rice
1 cup white wine (dry)
Pinch of saffron threads
1 ¼ cup onion, chopped
1 cup parmesan cheese, divided ½ cup shredded,
 ½ cup grated
2 tablespoons unsalted butter

2 tablespoons clarified butter
1 clove garlic, minced
1½ tablespoons garlic infused olive oil
1½ tablespoons fresh parsley, chopped
2 tablespoons of chives, chopped
½ teaspoon dried oregano
Zest of 1 lemon
Kosher salt
Fresh ground black pepper
Garnish with scallions

## Method of Preparation

1. Pour the white wine into a bowl and add a pinch of the saffron. Set aside.
2. Heat 2 large Dutch ovens on the stove. To one pot add the broth and water and bring to a slight boil. Reduce heat immediately but keep hot. To the other pot add the olive oil and unsalted butter.
3. Heat the shrimp in the oil and unsalted butter until opaque but not fully cooked. About 2 minutes. Remove with a slotted spoon.
4. Add the clarified butter. When hot, add onions and cook until translucent; then add garlic being careful not to burn the garlic. Cook for 1-2 minutes more.
5. Add the salt and rice stirring constantly and being sure to coat each grain.
6. Pour in the white wine/saffron mixture and oregano. Continue stirring until all the wine is absorbed. Be careful the rice does not stick to bottom of pot. Do this for 3 minutes.
7. Add the broth, ½ to ¾ cup at a time, stirring constantly. As the broth evaporates add the next ½ cup of broth. Continue this until the risotto is very creamy and most of the broth has been used.
8. Fold in the shredded parmesan a little at a time checking for creaminess. If desired, add the grated parmesan (a little at a time). Turn burner off and remove pot from heat.
9. Off heat, add the parsley, chives, and lemon zest to the risotto and stir. Fold in the shrimp, langoustine and more broth as needed. Adjust seasoning with salt and pepper.

Saffron is one of the most expensive spices, by weight, in the world so use wisely and knowledgably. To get the most out of your saffron threads and pull out its flowery pungent taste and beautiful orange color, soak the saffron in water or white wine.
About 20 saffron threads equal a pinch, so don't over do it.

# Vegetable, Cheese & Tomato Tart

## Ingredients

1 red bell pepper, large dice
1 green bell pepper, large dice
1 yellow bell pepper, large dice
1 medium red onion, large dice
1 medium eggplant, large dice
2 carrots
1 small sweet potato
½ butternut squash, large dice
3-4 shallots, chopped
7 cherry tomatoes, halved
½ teaspoon marjoram

4 sprigs of fresh thyme
1 cup heavy cream
2 eggs
½ cup ricotta
½ cup parmesan, grated
½ cup feta
Kosher salt
Fresh ground black pepper
½ teaspoon cumin
1 teaspoon turmeric
2 pie crusts

## Method of Preparation

1. Preheat oven to 425°.
2. First, blind bake the crust. To do this, cover the pie crust with parchment paper and place the item(s) you will use to add weight to the pie crust. I use dried beans. Bake for about 15 to 17 minutes. After 15 minutes remove the beans and return crust to oven to finish in about another 5 minutes or until the crust golden brown. Set aside to cool.
3. Next, in a large bowl add the squash, sweet potato and carrots. Add a little salt, pepper, marjoram and a little oil and toss. Place vegetables on a parchment lined baking sheet and bake until done.
4. In the same bowl, mix the peppers and red onion adding a little salt, pepper, marjoram and a little infused oil. Mix to coat all the vegetables. Pour onto a lined baking sheet and bake until done.
5. In the same large bowl, add the eggplant, turmeric, cumin, salt, pepper and a little oil. Mix together and lay eggplant flat on a lined baking sheet. Don't put it in the oven just yet. Season the halved tomatoes with salt, pepper and a little oil. Add to the same baking sheet as the eggplant and bake until done. Remove when done and allow to cool.
6. Heat a skillet and drizzle with oil. Add the shallots and cook until soft and tender. Remove.
7. In a separate bowl add the cheeses and mix.
8. Now to fill the cooled pie crust, spread cooled shallots along the bottom of each pie crust. Top with a mixture of the root vegetables, pepper medley and eggplant. Sprinkle with fresh thyme leaves.
9. Take a spoon and drop chunks of the cheese on top of the vegetables.
10. Lay the halved tomatoes, open side up, onto the cheese.
11. Whisk the eggs, heavy cream and pepper together in a bowl.
12. Pour the egg mixture into the pans. Shake the crust so the mixture fills in all the nooks and crannies. Sprinkle again with fresh thyme leaves and pepper.
13. Bake at 325° for 35 to 40 minutes. Check the crust, if the crust is okay continue baking for an additional 10-15 minutes. If the crust looks too dark, cover the edges with foil and continue baking until a toothpick comes out clean or the center of the tart is not jiggly.

# Roasted Cauliflower & Quinoa Salad

2 cups cooked quinoa
2 heads cauliflower, cut like steaks
1 cup cauliflowerettes chopped
1/2 cup roasted peppers, chopped
1 cucumber, diced
1 sweet potato, diced, roasted and pureed
1 small red onion, diced
6 cherry tomatoes, halved
Fresh ground black pepper

Kosher salt
Chimichurri Sauce
8 ounces fresh baby spinach
1/8 teaspoons lemon juice
1 teaspoon marjoram
Extra virgin olive oil
Balsamic Vinaigrette

## Method of Preparation

1. Remove the outer parts of the cauliflower heads. Cut the bottom to sit the head flat.
2. With head up cut from top to bottom in 1/2 - 1/3 inch thick steak pieces. Steaks should remain intact.
3. Lay steaks on parchment lined baking sheet. Drizzle lemon juice on steaks. Season with salt, pepper, turmeric and marjoram.
4. Drizzle with olive oil.
5. Heat skillet and sear steaks on both sides and return to baking sheet. When all steaks are seared, finish in a 350°F preheated oven until tender, about 10-12 minutes.
6. Cook quinoa according to package directions. Be sure to rinse quinoa under water for 3 minutes swirling around to remove any unseen residue prior to cooking.
7. In a pan heat a drizzle of olive oil. Sauté chopped cauliflowerettes and onions until onions are translucent. Remove to a large bowl.
8. Add peppers, cucumbers, tomatoes and cooked quinoa to the bowl. Season with salt and pepper. Toss and set aside.
9. In a separate bowl gently toss spinach with your favorite balsamic vinaigrette.
10. To serve : Brush plate with Chimichurri Sauce. Place spinach in the center of plate. Top with quinoa salad. Add a cauliflower steak and garnish with sweet potato purée.

# Vegetables & Sides

Macaroni & Cheese 95

Carrot Soufflé 96

Collard Greens with Smoked Turkey 98

Collard Greens with Sun-Dried Tomatoes & Garlic 98

Farro with Vegetables 100

Spinach Cranberry Rice 102

Vegetable Sauté  104

Roasted Gold Potatoes 10

Truffle Fries 108

Glazed Carrots 110

## Macaroni and Cheese

Ingredients

1 pound elbow pasta
1 stick of butter
3 tablespoons all-purpose flour
1/4 quarter cup Swiss cheese
4 cups of milk, plus extra
1/4 cup of sour cream

Turmeric
2 cups of sharp chedder cheese
Pinch of cayenne
½ teaspoon salt
Fresh ground black pepper

Method of Preparation

1. Cook elbow pasta according to package directions. Add tumeric to water.
   Strain reserving 1/2 cup of pasta water and set aside.
2. In the same pot used for the pasta add butter and melt.
   Whisk in the flour and continue whisking to avoid any lumps.
3. Add the milk and continue whisking until thickened.
4. Add salt, pepper, pinch of cayenne, chedder cheese and sour cream.
5. Using a wooden spoon stir until all the cheese is melted and incorporated.
6. Return pasta to the pot and mix thoroughly.
7. In a buttered cast iron skillet, pour cheesy pasta and top with Swiss cheese (if desired) and bake at 350° for 20 to 25 minutes or until the cheese is bubbling on the sides and browned on top.

Note: If cheese sauce is too thick, add more pasta water. Enjoy!

# Carrot Soufflé

## Ingredients

2 pounds of carrots
3 tablespoons all-purpose flour
3 large eggs, lightly beaten
2 tablespoons butter
2 mint leaves
1 teaspoon baking powder

1 teaspoon powdered sugar
1 teaspoon vanilla extract
2/3 cup granulated sugar
1/4 teaspoon salt
Pinch of ground cardamom
Pinch of cinnamon
1/4 cup fat-free sour cream
Cooking spray

## Method of Preparation

1.   Preheat oven to 350°.
2.   In a large stock pot bring carrots to a boil until very tender.
     Drain and place into a food processor. Add sugar and process until smooth.
3.   In a separate bowl add flour, baking powder, salt, cinnamon and cardamom.
     Mix together. Add to processor.
4.   Melt butter in microwave with mint leaves. Remove and discard leaves.
5.   Add sour cream and butter and process until smooth.
6.   In a separate bowl, beat eggs until fluffy and fold into the carrot mixture.
7.   Spray a baking dish with nonstick cooking spray and spoon mixture into dish.
8.   Bake at 350° for 45 to 55 minutes. Edges should be slightly brown and soufflé
     puffed and set on top.
9.   Remove from oven, sprinkle with powdered sugar and serve immediately.

# Collard Greens with Smoked Turkey
(Southern Style)

Ingredients

2 large bunches of collards, stems removed
3 quarts of water
2 cups chicken broth
1¼ - 1½ lbs. smoked turkey
1 tablespoon kosher salt
1 tablespoon sugar
1 teaspoon ground black pepper
1 teaspoon paprika

¼ cup canola oil
1 tablespoon extra virgin olive oil

Optional Ingredients
1 teaspoon cider vinegar
¼ teaspoon red pepper flakes

Method of Preparation
1. In a large Dutch oven (or other heavy bottom pot) add water, turkey, salt, sugar, pepper, paprika and oil. Bring to a boil. Cover, reduce heat and allow to cook for 40 minutes.
2. In the meantime, wash/rinse the collards very well.
3. If the stems are thick, remove them and chop collards into small pieces.
4. After about 35 minutes check the turkey and level of the "pot liquor." The liquid should have reduced by half and the turkey should be tender. If not, cook for another 10 minutes.
5. Add the stock and replace the lid. Cook for another 5 minutes just to raise the temperature back up.
6. Add the collards to the pot and sprinkle with a little more sugar, pinch of salt and drizzle of olive oil. Cover and cook for another 30-35 minutes or until tender and tasty.
7. Served best with cornbread.

# Collard Greens with Sun-Dried Tomatoes & Garlic

Ingredients

2 bunches of collards, stems removed
Olive oil
2 cloves garlic, sliced
¼ cup sun-dried tomatoes, chopped

Kosher salt
Fresh ground black pepper
1 tablespoon sugar
1 teaspoon of smoky paprika
¼ cup stock (vegetable)

Method of Preparation
1. Remove stems from collard greens. Rinse thoroughly to remove any soil.
2. Chop collards. Chop sun-dried tomatoes. Set aside.
3. Bring pot of salted water, paprika, pepper, sugar and 1 tablespoon of oil to a boil for 10 minutes.
4. Add collard greens and boil just until tender, another 10 to 15 minutes.
   In the last 3 or so minutes add the sun-dried tomatoes. Drain and rinse with cold water. Squeeze out excess water.
5. Drizzle oil in a saucepan.
6. Add garlic and cook for 1 minute watching carefully not to burn.
7. Add collards and tomatoes, stock and cook for 7 to 8 minutes. Adjust seasoning and enjoy!

# Farro with Vegetables

1 cup farro, rinsed thoroughly
2 cups chicken stock
1/3 cup dried cherries, chopped
4 cloves garlic, roasted
1 cup cherry tomatoes, halved
½ cauliflower, florets only
2 mini bell peppers, red & orange, diced
1 mini yellow bell pepper, halved

1 medium red onion, divided
2 small zucchinis, cut bite-sized pieces
1 jalapeno, seeded and diced
½ small red cabbage, cut
2-3 variety of small potatoes, diced
1 small sweet potato, diced
Olive oil for drizzling
Kosher salt
Fresh ground black pepper
1 rosemary sprig

Method of Preparation

1. Heat a large pot on the stove with chicken stock. Bring to a boil.
2. Rinse farro under cold water several times removing any debris and coatings that may be on the grain. Add to the stock.
3. Add rosemary and cherries and stir. Bring back to a boil, then reduce heat to simmer and cover until done.
4. While farro is cooking, sauté vegetables individually so they each retain their color.
5. First sauté all the onions. Remove 1/3 and add to the farro.
   Leave remaining onions in the pan.
6. Add cabbage to the pan and cook. Remove when it is slightly tender and set aside.
7. Next, sauté peppers. Remove. Set aside. Add tomatoes and cook for 2 minutes. Remove. Set aside.
8. Add zucchini and jalapeno and sauté. Remove and set aside.
9. Drizzle oil and sauté potatoes. Cook until browned and still slightly firm.
10. Mix farro with all the vegetables. Add salt and pepper to taste.

*This is great for vegetarians, but chicken, steak, seafood or even avocado can be added. I topped mine with goat cheese and a drizzle of balsamic glaze!*

# Spinach Cranberry Rice

Ingredients
5 cups of fresh spinach, chopped
2 cups cooked rice
1 medium onion, diced
1 tablespoon olive oil
½ cup chicken broth
½ cup dried cranberries
Optional: Sliced almonds

Method of Preparation
1. In a large pan drizzle olive oil and sauté onions for 2-3 minutes.
2. Add cranberries to the pan and allow to plump a bit.
3. Add the cooked rice and a little chicken broth (a little at a time) as needed to produce steam to heat the rice. Stir.
4. Season rice with salt and pepper. Add spinach and toss to combine.
5. Top with almonds if desired.

# Bulgur Wheat Pilaf

Ingredients
1 cup bulgur wheat, toasted
2 cups vegetable stock
½ cup fresh parsley, chopped
2 garlic cloves, minced
4½ ounces baby portabella mushrooms, sliced
3 cherry tomatoes, halved
1 medium onion, small dice
1 teaspoon coconut oil
2 teaspoons lemon juice
¾ teaspoon kosher salt
Fresh ground black pepper, to taste
Optional : Pinenuts, toasted

Method of Preparation
1. Heat oil in a saucepan and sauté the onions and garlic.
2. Add the mushrooms and cook until tender.
3. Add the bulgur and stock to the pan and bring to a slight boil.
4. Reduce heat and simmer uncovered for 15 minutes or until the bulgur is cooked.
5. Remove from heat and fluff with a fork.
6. Toss the pilaf with the parsley, tomatoes, lemon juice, salt and pepper. Serve.
7. Optional: Top with pinenuts if desired.

# Vegetable Sauté

1 whole zucchini, batonnet cut
1 carrot, batonnet cut
Bell pepper variety (red, green, yellow and orange), thick strips
Kosher salt
Fresh ground black pepper
½ teaspoon dried marjoram
Coconut oil
Optional: Red onion, cut into thick strips

Method of Preparation
1. In a large bowl combine all the vegetables.
2. Sprinkle with salt, pepper and marjoram. Toss to combine.
3. Add a little coconut oil to a large sauté pan. When melted add the vegetables and sauté until brightly colored and tender.
4. Garnish with fresh herbs and enjoy!

This is a very, very easy way to add color to your plate and to use leftover vegetables in the refrigerator. Sometimes I have a carrot lying around, one last stalk of celery and maybe a forgotton squash or onion. Vegetable sauté is my go to color side dish and I eat it for breakfast, lunch, dinner or as a snack.

# Roasted Gold Potatoes

Ingredients
3 pounds gold potatoes
¼ cup of garlic infused olive oil
1 teaspoon kosher salt
¾ teaspoon fresh ground pepper
1¼ tablespoon fresh parsley, chopped
1 tablespoon unsalted butter
Optional: 1 tablespoon parmesan, grated

Method of Preparation
1. Preheat the oven to 400°
2. Scrub potatoes clean and pat dry. Cut into large chunks and place in a bowl.
3. Add olive oil, salt and pepper. Toss to coat.
4. Transfer potatoes to a lined baking sheet in a single layer.
5. Roast in the oven for 40–45 minutes checking and tossing around every 10 or so minutes. Cook until browned.
6. In a bowl combine the butter and parsley. Set aside.
7. Remove potatoes from oven and dump into the butter bowl. Toss to coat.
8. Return potatoes to the baking sheet and oven for 2 minutes to dry. Remove and serve hot. Top with cheese if desired.

# Truffle Fries

Ingredients
4 gold potatoes, cut into ¼ to 1/3 inch thick cut fries
1½ tablespoon truffle oil
1½ tablespoon fresh parsley, chopped
Kosher salt
Fresh ground black pepper
Pinch of red pepper flakes,
Optional: 2-3 tablespoons parmesan, grated

Method of Preparation
1. Preheat oven to 425°.
2. Line a baking sheet with parchment paper and set aside.
3. In a large bowl add the potatoes. Sprinkle with salt, pepper and drizzle with truffle oil. Toss to coat.
4. Spread the potatoes in a single layer on a prepared baking sheet and bake for 35 to 45 minutes or until golden brown. (Shake the pan periodically to turn potatoes over.)
5. Remove from the oven and toss with parsley, parmesan, and if using, the red pepper flakes.
6. Serve with a your favorite dipping sauce or my Creamy Chipotle Sauce (see index).

# Glazed Carrots

Ingredients:
3 medium carrots, peeled, batonnet cut (like French fries!)
2 tablespoons agave nectar
1 mint sprig, whole
3 tablespoons water
¼ teaspoon kosher salt
Pinch of cayenne
Coconut oil
Optional: Toasted pecans

Method of Preparation:
1. In a wide sauté pan add the oil and heat.
2. Add carrots and 2 tablespoons of water to the pan.
   Cook until water evaporates.
3. Add salt, agave and mint. Stir and cook for an additional 3 to 4 minutes coating all the carrots.
4. Add the remaining water and cover. Steam until the carrots are tender.
5. Remove lid and discard the mint. Allow any remaining water to evaporate.
   Serve hot with pecans if desired

# Sauces, Vinaigrettes & Condiments

# Cranberry-Orange Sauce

## Ingredients
10 ounces of 100% cranberry juice
2 tablespoons of orange marmalade
2 tablespoons habanero sauce (or other thick sauce with a kick)
2 cloves of garlic, crushed
¼ cup of dried cranberries
1 tablespoon of water (plus extra if needed)
2 ounces of orange juice
Fresh orange slices for garnish

## Method of Preparation
1. Place cranberry juice, marmalade, habanero sauce, garlic, cranberries and water into a sauce pan. Boil and reduce by half. Stir and set aside. Mixture will thicken upon resting.
2. Remove ¼ up to half of the sauce and reserve for serving with prepared protein.
3. Use the remaining sauce to baste your protein as it cooks.
   Note: If sauce thickens too much, use orange juice a little at a time in the sauce until desired consistency

# Lemon-Honey Dijon Vinaigrette

## Ingredients
1/3 cup fresh squeezed lemon juice
2 tablespoons cider vinegar
1 small shallot, chopped
2 1/2 teaspoons dijon mustard
2 tablespoons honey
1 cup extra virgin olive oil
Kosher salt
Fresh ground black pepper

## Method of Preparation
1. Place shallots, mustard, lemon juice, honey and cider into a food processor. Process.
2. Slowly add oil until smooth and slightly creamy.
3. Season with salt and pepper. Enjoy!

# Garlic-Dill Yogurt Sauce

1 cup low-fat plain Greek yogurt
2 tablespoons extra-virgin olive oil
2 garlic cloves, minced
2 lime wedges
1 tablespoon shallot, diced
3/4 teaspoon salt
½ teaspoon honey
½ teaspoon dried dill weed
3 to 4 tablespoons water, as needed
Fresh ground pepper, as needed
Pinch of red pepper flakes (optional)

Method of Preparation
1. In a small pan, drizzle a little oil. Sauté shallots and garlic.
2. Squeeze juice of lime wedges into pan.
3. Add 2 tablespoons of water and remove from heat.
4. Add all the remaining ingredients in a bowl and stir.
5. Combine the shallot mixture and stir.
6. Pour mixture into a blender (or a Nutri-bullet) and process until desired consistency.
7. Use as a dip or add more water to loosen, adjust seasoning and use as a dressing.

# Triple Berry Sauce

Ingredients

Ingredients
½ cup blackberries
½ cup blueberries
½ cup raspberries
¼ cup sugar plus 1 tablespoon
Zest of 1 lemon
2 teaspoons fresh squeezed lemon juice
¼ cup grand marnier
1 tablespoon pure maple syrup

Method of Preparation
1. Place all ingredients except lemon zest in a pot or saucepan. Bring to a slight boil. Reduce heat and simmer until about ½ sauce remains (or coats the back of a spoon).
2. Remove from heat and add in zest. Stir and taste. Mixture will thicken upon sitting.
3. Serve and enjoy.

# Orange Sauce

Ingredients
Zest of 1 orange
½ cup fresh squeezed orange juice
4 orange segments, reserve remaining for garnish
1 tablespoon fresh squeezed lemon juice
½ cup Cointreau
½ cup sugar
2 tablespoons of clarified butter

Method of Preparation
1. Place all ingredients in a saucepan. Bring to a slight boil. Reduce heat and simmer until about ½ of sauce remains or the sauce coats back of a spoon and stays.
2. Remove from heat and stir in zest a little at a time until desired flavor is reached.
3. Mixture will continue to thicken upon sitting. Serve warm.

# Mushroom & Shallot Sauce

## Ingredients
2 tablespoons melted butter
1 tablespoon garlic infused extra virgin olive oil
1 shallot, chopped
1 pint of mushrooms, sliced, reserve 2 whole
2 garlic clove, finely chopped
Chicken broth, as needed
½ teaspoon dijon mustard
½ teaspoon Worcestershire sauce
2 tablespoons chives
1/3 cup heavy cream
Kosher salt
Fresh ground black pepper

## Method of Preparation
Heat a little butter and oil in the pan. Add the shallot and sauté. Add garlic and sliced mushrooms and continue cooking for about 2 minutes. Pour in a little chicken broth. Allow broth to evaporate completely. In a separate bowl, whisk mustard and Worcestershire sauce. Add a little broth and whisk. Pour into pan. Cook for about a minute more and then add the heavy cream and chives. Season with salt and pepper and allow to reduce and thicken.

# Cognac Prune Dressing

## Ingredients
Avocado or extra-virgin olive oil
1 shallot, finely chopped
3 sprigs of fresh thyme
12 prunes, pitted, chopped
1 teaspoon dark molasses
1/3 cup all natural grape juice
1/3 cup of vegetable broth
2 ounces of Cognac
2 tablespoons water
Kosher salt, to taste
Fresh ground pepper, to taste

## Method of Preparation
1. Heat a large pan and drizzle with oil.
2. Add the shallots and stir until soft.
3. Add the thyme, prunes, molasses and grape juice and reduce heat to medium. Keep an eye on the mixture and stir. Once prunes become soft and plump remove from heat.
4. Off heat add in the broth and cognac. Stir together.
5. Season with salt and pepper and allow to cool.
6. Place cooled ingredients in a blender and process until smooth. If dressing is too thick, add water a tablespoon at a time until desired consistency. If you should add too much, simply plump up a few more prunes and add them to the blender.

Note: I use the thickened version as a healthy dip!

## Easy Buttermilk Ranch Dressing

Ingredients
¾ to 1 cup of buttermilk
1 to 2 tablespoons of mayonnaise
Fresh ground black pepper
Pinch or two of salt
1/2 teaspoon of chopped parsley
1 packet of Buttermilk Ranch seasoning mix

Method of Preparation
    Whisk or stir all the ingredients together until well blended. Done!

# Creamy Chipotle Sauce

½ cup plain yogurt
½ cup mayonnaise
3 tablespoons fresh cilantro, chopped
2 tablespoons fresh lime juice
Zest of lime, to taste
1 chipotle pepper in adobe sauce
2 roasted garlic cloves
1 tablespoon honey
Kosher Salt, to taste
Fresh ground pepper (optional)

Method of Preparation
1.	Place all the ingredients into a food processor and blend.
2.	Put in a container and keep in the fridge.
Note: I use whole fat and fresh ingredients for full flavor, but feel free to adjust.

# Champagne Fig Dressing

Ingredients
4 tablespoons olive oil
1 teaspoon coriander
1 teaspoon dijon mustard
2 figs
½ lemon juice, plus extra
1 garlic clove, roasted
1 tablespoon Champagne vinegar
½ tablespoon honey
Kosher salt
Fresh ground black pepper
Champagne

Method of Preparation
1.	Combine first 8 ingredients in a food processor.
2.	Process until fully incorporated. Mixture will be thick and mildly lumpy.
3.	Add salt and pepper to taste.
4.	When ready for service, top off dressing with Champagne to desired consistency. (Adjust with salt and pepper as desired.)

# Spicy Remoulade Sauce

## Ingredients
½ cup sour cream
½ cup mayonnaise
2 tablespoon chipotle sauce (add 1 at a time)
1 tablespoon lime juice
½ cup fresh cilantro, divided (half chopped, half whole leaves)
½ teaspoon lime zest, to taste
Kosher salt
Fresh ground black pepper

## Method of Preparation
1. Mix together the sour cream, mayonnaise, lime juice, lime zest and chipotle sauce together.
2. Add salt and pepper to taste.
3. Fold in chopped cilantro. Use the remaining cilantro for garnish.

Note: 1 cup of Greek yogurt may be substituted for sour cream & mayonnaise.

A Sweet Ending: Cherry Choco Nana Cake

Layout & Design: Triumph Design

Photograph Credits: TRWphotos 20173740 series, istockphotos (#636137918, 484573122, 535398857, 177427379, 544598354, 543690852, 648085164, 489833495, 111979730, 64187610, 507125577, 486839918, 495472304, 186527681, 510015094, 173921403, 481054395, 468348156).

# About Chef Renee

Chef, Television Host, Cooking & Nutrition Instructor, Caterer, Speaker Chef Renée is a Connecticut resident of 26 years. Born and raised in Daytona Beach, Florida, she received her culinary degree from Johnson & Wales University and a B.S. from Florida Agricultural & Mechanical University. She stays busy as the owner of "Simply Chef Renée, LLC," a partner of "CDT Life's Energy, LLC," television host, cooking instructor, caterer and speaker of "All Things Food." This is her first cookbook and it's filled with a combination of colorful, nutritious and just plain good food.

Her career began long before she attended JWU and long before working at a Classic New England Inn where she continued her training after school. Her enthusiasm along with her love and compassion for people, good health and colorful food have gained her national attention and a loyal local following. She has been contacted by Food Network and other casting networks because of her dedication and commitment to education and training in the food industry.

Her show "Simply Fresh Food with Chef Renée" (now "Simply Chef Renée) was nominated for a National CATV Award which once again put her in the lime light. Renée enjoys her volunteer work and is committed to bringing cooking back into the kitchen and around the dinner table. Past work includes, radio talk show host, gift basket designer, teaching and (always) being a mom. When she is not cooking, you can find her in her beloved garden or wrapped up with a good book. She enjoys traveling and experiencing new food trends and different cultures which she incorporates into her repertoire of recipes.

simplychefrenee.com
Follow Chef Renée on Facebook & Instagram